Working with Ghanaians

Michael Creighton

Copyright © 2021 Michael Creighton

ISBN: 9798761362857

Kindle Edition License Notes:

Thank you for purchasing this book. This book remains the copyrighted property of the author, and may not be redistributed to others for commercial or non-commercial purposes. If you enjoyed this book, please encourage your friends to download or purchase their own copy from their favorite authorized retailer. Also, please leave a review for the book at your favourite retailer. Thank you for your support - *medase pa*!

Front cover image and design: Ngminvielu Kuuire

Praise for Working with Ghanaians

As a born and bred native Ghanaian, I can confidently endorse Michael, as the go-to person for any new visitor to my country, Ghana. For a person who first landed in Ghana as an exchange student, on a budget and then came back as a family man and a development expert, Michael is definitely not short of words for any subject matter on Ghana. This tells much of the in-depth knowledge of his rich Ghanaian experience.

Ndaase koraa Michael!

-Esenam Nyador, Miss Taxi Ghana

It is often said that Ghanaians are very warm and friendly people. There is no feeling more welcoming than to be the recipient of an enthusiastic "akwaaba" accompanied by a broad smile. But there is so much more to a cultural profile of a people than what might be expressed in a tourist pamphlet.

Michael Creighton's book takes the reader through an insightful and sensitive journey that explores the cultural context for effective negotiation, work relationships, business dealings and for managing service providers. He is uniquely qualified to lead us on this journey. Not only did he spend years in Ghana, he has viewed life in the country both from the backseat of a "trotro" as well as from the backseat of an air-conditioned V8 SUV. Both perspectives are real; but also serve as appropriate metaphors for viewing the culture across the full spectrum of society.

If you are planning a long stay in Ghana to study or work I strongly recommend this book. It is an enjoyable read but more important it also caters to the needs of people planning to work in Ghana including diplomats and senior executives who require a deeper and more nuanced appreciation of the cultural backdrop to their daily work experience. This important book is a must-read.

-Ronald E. Quist, CEO, Idilmat Ltd.

Running an office anywhere is challenging. As Ghana becomes an ever more important base for international business, diplomacy and civil society, Michael Creighton's book arrives full of stories and tips for expatriates who want to make their work life more productive as well as more enjoyable. Worth reading before you go and again after you've been at work there for a while.

-Darren Schemmer, former Canadian High Commissioner to Ghana

Table of Contents

A Very Large Disclaimer

Introduction 1
- Chale, Why This Book?
- "What Did You Bring Me?"
- What is Culture?
- What is Intercultural Learning?
- Intercultural Learning and Icebergs
- What is Ghanaian Culture?
- Staying Resilient in Ghana

Vignette #1: Wa, Upper West Region . . . 13

The Basics: Understanding Ghanaians and Their Cultures 15
- A Basic Cultural Profile
    - Ghanaians are social
    - Ghanaians are also communal
    - Ghanaians are harmonious
    - Ghanaians are also tangential
    - Ghanaians are proud
    - Ghanaians are also hierarchical
    - Ghanaians are spiritual
    - Ghanaians are also religious
- Other Important Cultural Attitudes
    - Gender Roles
    - Short-Term vs Long-Term Thinking
    - Accra vs Everywhere Else
    - The Hustle: Nobody Has Just One Job
    - GMT: Ghana Maybe Time
    - Cultural Rituals: Weddings, Outdoorings and Funerals

- ° Property and Ownership
- ° Service
- ° Maintenance
- ° Cultural Translators

How Ghanaians Understand Foreigners . . 41
- Businesspeople
- Diplomats
- Development Workers
- Missionaries
- Tourists
- How Ghanaians Hear Foreigners
- How Ghanaians See Foreigners
- Bringing It All Together

Vignette #2: Shopping Mall, Accra . . . 53

Money Matters 55
- How Ghanaians See Money – The Art of the Hustle
- Ghanaian Networks
- Some Things Have Value, Others Do Not
- Strategic Delaying
- Credit Traps
- Watching Your Money

Negotiation 63
- Negotiation: an Essential Skill
- The Art of the Haggle
- Positions of Strength and Weakness
- Negotiation at the Organizational Level
- So How Do You Negotiate in Ghana?
- Next Steps: Using Your Intercultural Skills in Ghana

Establishing an Organization 71
- Making a Plan and Sequencing
- Shiny Things vs. Needed Things
- Finding Space
- Finding People
- Hiring
- Now that Everything Is in Place

Managing and Leading Ghanaians . . . 79
- Setting Expectations
- Managing Styles in Ghana
- Building a Team
- Motivating Your Team
- Autonomy and Proactivity
- Time Management
- Working Remotely
- Getting and Giving Feedback
- Resolving Conflict
- Building Integrity and Avoiding Corruption in Your Organization
- Firing
- A Final Note: Choose Your Battles Wisely

Doing Business with Ghanaians . . . 97
- The Power of Relationships
- Greetings
- Meetings
- Speeches and Presentations
- Workshops, Training and Conferences
- Learning the Language
- Working with Government and Bureaucracy
- Gift, Dash or Bribe?

Vignette #3: Kumasi, Ashanti Region . . 109

Building Bridges 111
- Many Friends on Paper
- Ways to Build Bridges
- Easy Things
- Not-So-Easy Things
- Hard Things
- A Few Shortcuts

Afterword: Ezekiel's Haircut . . . 121

Annex: Working With… . . . 123
- Cleaners
- Cooks and Caterers
- Househelp
- Gardeners
- Mechanics
- Handymen
- Servers and Sales Associates
- Tailors and Seamstresses
- Drivers
- Security Guards
- Movers

Acknowledgements and Resources . . 137

A Very Large Disclaimer

This book was primarily written by a foreigner. Thus, it bears the worldview of a white, Western male. However, I have developed my understanding over several years spent living in Ghana as a university student and professional, including trips throughout via trotro, taxi, intercity bus and the occasional ferry and in observing and talking to countless Ghanaians from cocoa farmers to government ministers.

This book is also informed by Ghanaian and non-Ghanaian colleagues who have anonymously shared their experiences and opinions, which vary greatly. Furthermore, I am not a professor, nor a sociologist in any technical sense of the term. Where I have tried to explain universal phenomena, I have relied on the works of people more intelligent than me and have tried to credit them accordingly.

Taking the advice I dispense further in the book, I have taken an intercultural learning approach and have tried to remove my cultural blinders and look beyond my own worldview to try and understand Ghanaians. As you will read, understanding your own cultural biases is crucial to understanding and appreciating Ghanaian culture.

I use the terms "Ghanaian", "Ghanaians" and "Ghanaian culture" as generalizations, though even using these terms are massive oversimplifications as there is no single type of Ghanaian or Ghanaian culture: a Ghanaian can be a rural Muslim Dagomba-speaking farmer with two wives and a flock of guinea fowl living on the Sahel, or a wealthy evangelical preacher and businessman at a megachurch in suburban Accra. A Ghanaian can be an animist Fante fisherman living in a stilt house in Nzulezo, Western Region or an Ashanti market queen selling textiles in the warrens of Kejetia in Kumasi. That Ghana has developed a common national identity in six decades of existence is a massive achievement.

I am not a Ghanaian and as such, I am not capable of telling Ghanaian stories or speaking on behalf of Ghanaians. My intended audience is non-Ghanaians. As such, I have tried to write in a style that communicates the experience of a non-Ghanaian operating within Ghanaian culture to other non-Ghanaians, including challenges and frustrations. Some may find this problematic. However, my goal is to decode Ghanaian culture so that non-Ghanaians can better understand it, appreciating both the commonalities and differences. At all times, I have tried to speak as someone who appreciates the rich cultures of Ghana and who has great affection for Ghanaians. Any errors are thus my own. I encourage more people to write about this, especially Ghanaians. We collectively must encourage and amplify Ghanaian voices in this conversation.

In short: Sorry-oo[1]

Until the lion learns to speak, the story of the hunt will glorify the hunter.

-African proverb (probably not Ghanaian)

---

[1] *Sorry-oo*, pronounced "Sorry oh" is the style of a Ghanaian apology, but also a polite lamentation for the misfortune of others. For example, if your car breaks down or your child falls, a Ghanaian will respond *Sorry-oo!*

Introduction

Tens of thousands of foreigners live, study and work in Ghana, including diplomats, non-governmental organization (NGO) workers, venture capitalists, missionaries and corporate executives – and their spouses and children. Many thrive and some stay for the rest of their lives, enjoying fruitful careers and personal lives while contributing to Ghana's social and economic development. Why is this? It is not about how they handle the heat, nor the humidity, nor their affinity for fufu, but rather how well they work and live with Ghanaians.

Many others have difficult experiences living and working in Ghana and are unable to navigate and adapt to life in Ghana. This leads to frustration and sours things on a personal and professional level as well as for organizations. Companies and NGOs invest heavily and risk failure without understanding the cultural terrain. At worst, people leave Ghana with regressive attitudes on Ghanaians and their culture, deterring others from exploring opportunities and investing. Would it not have been better if these people had a better understanding beforehand?

Chale[2], Why This Book?

This book is different from travel guide books like the *Bradt's Ghana* by Philip Briggs or *Ghana – Culture Smart!: The Essential Guide to Customs & Culture* by Ian Utley. These are excellent books on Ghana and it is strongly recommend that you read these first to give you an overview of Ghana and its cultures. There are also

---

[2] *Chale* is a corruption of *Charlie*, local slang for *friend*.

resources for preparing to live in Ghana, including *Your Essential Guide on Moving to Ghana* by Ivy Prosper and *No Worries – the Essential Guide to Living in Ghana* by the North American Women's Association. These books will lay the foundation for living in Ghana and they as well as other resources are listed at the end of the book.

This book is also different from investment guides as it does not address the technical aspects of specific industries, but is generalized so that however you plan to work or invest *in* Ghana, you have an idea of how to work *with* Ghanaians[3].

Getting beyond pleasantries and understanding how to get things done, there's a much deeper aspect to interacting with Ghanaians: how to understand what they are (and are not) saying and how to more effectively conduct business with them. Professionals from all walks of life arrive in Ghana with a limited understanding of the culture and due to the steep learning curve, they lose months of productivity, stress needlessly and end up with negative experiences. This book intends to fill this gap.

"What Did You Bring Me?"

Over drinks, a foreign office manager lamented to a fellow colleague at his office. "Every time I come back from holiday feeling refreshed and energized and as soon as I return, instead of welcoming me and asking me how it was, they say, *So what did you bring me?* Can you believe it? How insulting! In my culture, you don't just ask for something like that. You know, I don't feel I can trust my workers when they go around openly looking for gifts."

---

[3] For sector-specific information, contact your embassy or high commission's trade commissioner, commercial service or trade office, or your country's own local Ghanaian business association or chamber of commerce.

Later on at the office, the colleague asked a Ghanaian worker about the manager. Instead of speaking about him, the Ghanaian said, "Do you remember the previous manager? She was loved by everyone and she really understood us. Whenever she came back from her home country, she brought a box of cookies for the office. That's so important that whenever you travel, you bring a gift, just a little something to show respect. If I ever came home from a conference without a gift for family and friends, I would be in such trouble!"

So a box of cookies is not really just a box of cookies at this office, but so much more: it represents community, harmony and respect. All of these are hallmarks of Ghanaian culture. But how could a foreigner understand that any of this is important for his office? It all comes down to understanding how culture works.

What is Culture?

In short, culture is the social behaviour and norms found in human societies – how people organize their lives and understand their environments. Concretely, culture is what we do, think and feel. Culture is expressed through food, music, literature, visual arts, architecture, language, religion, social rituals and clothing and in other areas as well[4]. Culture is shared between and transmitted over time by people. Culture is fluid and changes from place to place and from generation to generation, evolving over time. Cultures overlap and have sub-cultures within themselves. Related to the earlier disclaimer, there's no single definition of "Ghanaian" culture.

---

[4] This is borrowing heavily from the definition provided by the Canadian Foreign Service Institute's Centre for Intercultural Learning. Also: *Kuada, John and Yao Chachah. Ghana: Understanding the People and Their Culture. Woeli, 1999*

What is Intercultural Learning?

First off, consider: why read a book about how to work with Ghanaians? Quite simply, because Ghanaian culture and your culture have some significant differences as well as similarities that may not be immediately apparent. These can cause serious friction if one does not recognize them and understand how to navigate cultural differences and harness the similarities. This is what is called "intercultural learning".

Intercultural Learning and Icebergs

Consider two icebergs in the ocean[5]: viewed from afar, they appear to be two entirely separate and different entities floating freely. They are distinct, independent and distant.

Now look underneath the water: suddenly they are massive. Above the water, you could only see 10% of the structure. The other 90% was hidden. Furthermore, what appeared to be two very separate blocks of ice are actually much closer together under the water, maybe even touching or connected.

Cultures are like this as well. On the surface, there are many *visible symbols* of one's culture: clothing, food, music, manners, language and rituals. Hidden underneath are *unspoken rules* that are understood by people within the culture: etiquette, hierarchy and taboos. Even deeper are the *unconscious rules*: beliefs, values, experiences and collective history.

---

[5] If you live far from where icebergs are found, consider dropping two ice cubes in a glass of your favourite cold drink and watch them float mostly under the surface. Until you've finished your drink, that is.

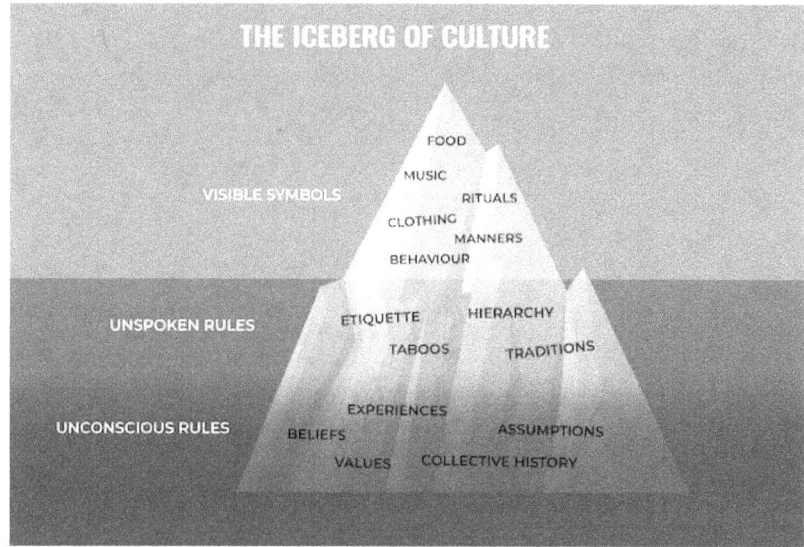

For example, kente cloth is a visible symbol of Ghanaian culture for Akans and Ewes. However, how kente is made, how it is worn, when it is worn and who can wear it are not immediately visible to an outsider, but intrinsically understood by the locals as unspoken rules. Why kente is important in the first place, the emotional attachment locals have to it and the respect accorded to it historically are the unconscious rules. The idea of kente over time has changed as it is absorbed into modern fashion, design and advertising.

Most importantly, *your* culture is like this. What you visibly demonstrate is only a small part of your worldview, which is informed by deeply-held beliefs, social conditioning and traditions passed down from your ancestors. Beliefs of multiple cultures have contributed to your identity. While you may see most of your iceberg, people of other cultures only see a small part of it.[6]

---

[6] Iceberg theory has its limitations. As a metaphor it only explains so much. Other cultural theories include onions with their many layers, programing software and goldfish in separate bowls. https://medium.com/@AFS/is-culture-like-an-onion-an-iceberg-or-some-kind-of-computer-software-c221df2292d4

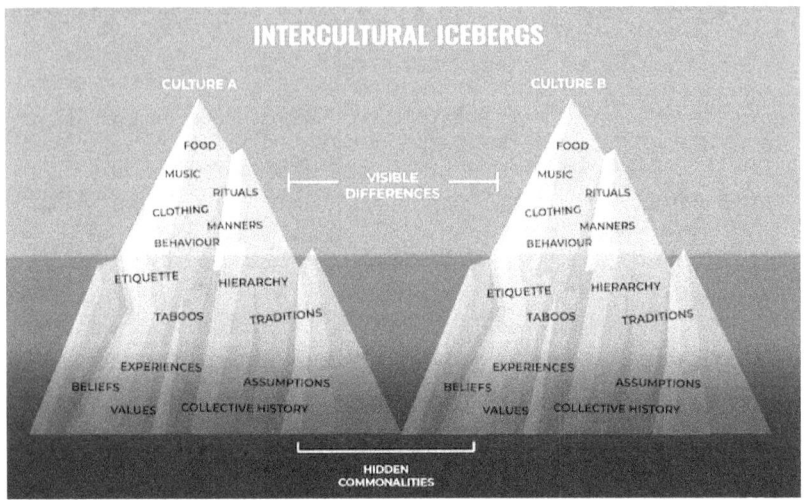

You may not even see parts of your own iceberg! This is a good time to think about your culture. Take some time to read about your own culture, absorb outside opinions and think about what shapes your own culture and beliefs, including what you take for granted. All of these things come from years (and generations) of lived experience. It is a humbling experience to think critically about this. Cultural anthropologists have concluded that there are as many normal ways of thinking and acting in the world as there are societies and one's own way of acting is not the only normal one[7], so there are a lot of icebergs out there. Understanding your iceberg will help you to decode other cultures[8].

This understanding of the self is part of "emotional intelligence", a set of skills that keeps you balanced and resilient in stressful situations. Moving to a foreign country and living within a foreign culture, while exciting, can be quite difficult in many ways, leading

---

[7] Kuada and Chachah. P. 1.
[8] An excellent resource is the Centre for Intercultural Learning, which includes cultural profiles of 118 countries, from the United States to Zimbabwe. https://www.international.gc.ca/cil-cai/country_insights-apercus_pays/countryinsights-apercuspays.aspx?lang=eng

to stress, anxiety and depression. Understanding yourself and your culture will help to keep you grounded in your own identity and to stay resilient[9].

An important part of this model is that the icebergs touch each other and could even be connected at times. This is where we find commonality and intercultural understanding. Relating with others requires a similar but distinct set of skills, called "social intelligence". Having this ability to read the feelings, emotions and actions of others will help to bridge the gap between cultures. In the words of Steven Covey, "Seek first to understand, then be understood,"[10] and ask questions whenever you can. Throughout the book, there will be strategies to make connections and also to find common bonds and interests, whether through music, food, or football.

Understanding these connections will allow you to live contentedly and work successfully in another culture as an "interculturally effective person".

Being an interculturally effective person is not a deeply technical exercise and nobody will give you a medal for it – but it does require serious critical thinking, self-reflection and a dose of humility. This may take some work, but the rewards will be great.

What is an interculturally effective person?

---

[9] Janssen, Linda A. *The Emotionally Resilient Expat.* Summertime Publishing, 2013. P. 30-33. Overall a great resource on living abroad as an expat, covering a wide variety of topics and pulling together additional resources.

[10] Covey, Steven. *The Seven Habits of Highly Effective People.* FranklinCovey. 2013. P. 249. A perennial bestseller, this book can be a useful management tool for work and life and may also speak to entrepreneurial-minded and religious Ghanaians.

Someone who is interculturally effective has three main attributes:

1) an ability to communicate with people of another culture in a way that earns their respect and trust, thereby encouraging a cooperative and productive workplace that is conducive to the achievement of professional or assignment goals;

2) the capacity to adapt his/her professional skills (both technical and managerial) to fit local conditions and constraints; and

3) the capacity to adjust personally so that s/he is content and generally at ease in the host culture.

In sum, although the skills of the individuals do not guarantee success, without these skills overall success of international and intercultural projects or assignments will rarely, if ever, be achieved. They are a necessary condition of success.

-*A Profile of the Interculturally Effective Person, the Centre for Intercultural Learning*

What is most important is for you as a reader to understand:

1) Culture is what we do, think and feel. You have culture. Ghanaians have culture;

2) Respect the differences between your culture and Ghanaian culture and people;

3) You can work through the differences between cultures; and

4) You will be all the happier for it.

What is Ghanaian Culture?

As noted earlier, there's no single Ghanaian culture and great diversity among communities within Ghana. However, we can take some shortcuts to help us understand commonalities that are found throughout the peoples of Ghana.

First: **Ghanaians are social and communal.** No man or woman in Ghana is an island. Social networks are critical to everyday living and working and decisions are made not only for the individual, but for others as well.

Second: **Ghanaians are harmonious and tangential.** Within these social networks, Ghanaians seek to ensure that there is a balance in social relations and will go to great lengths to avoid giving offense, disrespect or disappointment, often using coded and indirect language to make their point.

Third: **Ghanaians are proud and hierarchical.** In spite of the communal and harmonious spirit, Ghanaians have a strong understanding of identity and in Ghanaian society, everyone has their place.

Fourth: **Ghanaians are spiritual and religious.** For Ghanaians, nothing happens by chance and everything happens for a reason. The Almighty has the final decision on all things, which must be respected and recognized.

These traits will appear throughout the book to remind the reader that Ghanaians have a strong culture that informs their day-to-day lives, including in business. By recognizing these traits, one can identify them and learn how to more effectively work interculturally with Ghanaians.

Staying Resilient in Ghana

Working with Ghanaians

Many foreigners will experience working in Ghana as an adventure and a challenge – but also at times it is a struggle mentally, emotionally and physically.

Consider two expats spending their last night in Accra after long stays in Ghana. One heads to a popular local jazz club with Ghanaian and expat friends to enjoy a Club beer, kebabs with suya spice and enjoy a live performance by an Afrobeat legend. The other has a quiet house party with other expats, listening to western pop hits and drinking the last of their Heineken. What do these two nights say about the experiences of the expats respectively? Which one is more likely to have stayed emotionally resilient and integrated the most into Ghanaian culture? Which one was more likely to have experienced success working with Ghanaians?

It is worth taking a moment to think about the challenge of working in another culture. There are the classic stages of culture shock: the excitement of change, honeymoon, frustration, adjustment and acceptance. This happens for anyone moving between cultures – and can include a reverse culture shock upon return to one's home country. Ghana is no exception. Whether coming from the Netherlands or Nigeria, there is some level of shock.

Remember that everyone has a culture. This culture informs one's identity, which is the perception of the self. It helps us know who we are. It changes over time, but it anchors us through periods of change and struggle.

Culture in Ghana is very strong, which can overwhelm some foreigners and lead to difficulties in reconciling their own culture and personal identity with their personal circumstances and surroundings. How can one stay grounded and confident in their own identity? In short, it requires physical and emotional resilience, including the ability to recover from and/or adjust to negative events or significant change[11].

Working with Ghanaians

Resilience is what underpins the success of entrepreneurs and the sustainable results of development workers in Ghana. It also keeps people cool as they spend their sixth hour waiting at the immigration office.

While integrating into Ghanaian culture will certainly pay dividends for foreigners, it is not always possible. Forging deep emotional friendships and becoming a local can be difficult to achieve in Ghana. This leads to frustration. What is frustration? It is when one encounters the difference between their expectations and reality.

For this reason, you may find a source of resilience in your own culture. Maintaining one's identity may require connections with fellow expats and familiar things. This might include the occasional pizza order, a movie night or spending a little extra at the supermarket for a special treat from home. It may also include spending time with other expats or fellow nationals who can help you make sense of your experiences. If this is a source of strength and support, take this with you as you navigate Ghanaian culture.

Remember that you are not alone as a foreigner in Ghana. You are not the first and you will not be the last. So enjoy the experience, get to know the places and people and do enjoy the kebabs.

The one who asks questions does not lose his way.
-Akan proverb

It takes the moon more than one day to go around the earth.
-Akan proverb

---

[11] Janssen, 103

Working with Ghanaians

Vignette #1: Wa, Upper West Region

As a student at the University of Ghana, I took a bus with a friend across the country from Accra to Wa, a 13-hour journey. Arriving late in the evening, we were completely exhausted and in search of a hotel, with only basic guidebook info. A young man passing by on his bike stopped and approached us. He asked who we were, where we were from and where we were going. He offered to take us to the hotel and we all walked and talked together for some time. His name was Isaac and he was a student at St. John Secondary School. Once we arrived, he said goodbye and cycled off into the night.

We checked in and fell into a deep sleep. In the morning, the hotel manager informed us that Isaac had passed by on his way to school to check on us. Surprisingly, he never shared his phone number and unlike in Accra, there was no expectation of reciprocity. He simply wanted to help strangers who were a long way from home.

Isaac left an impression. It led me to wonder: who was this man? Why did he go out of his way to help us? What did he think of us? And what became of him? With so many questions, I clearly needed to understand this culture better.

Working with Ghanaians

The Basics: Understanding Ghanaians and Their Cultures

At first glance, an outsider may find Ghanaian culture and its manifestations very novel or even strange, but it is rooted in a logic and a lived experience that will make more sense with reflection.

First, consider a house. For western cultures, there is great pride in home ownership. How does one build a house? Most urban and suburban dwellers live in residential developments. A company purchases a large tract of land, plans a neighbourhood and drafts plans to sub-divide the land into lots connected by roads and utilities. The company then builds the neighbourhood in a few phases or all at once. Construction workers and contractors of all sorts are engaged: machine operators, asphalt layers, brick layers, plumbers, electricians, carpenters and drywall mechanics. After the construction period, the houses are ready for their owners who have purchased them with mortgages supplied by local banks. The homeowners take possession, move their families and their things in and live their lives as happy residents, slowly paying off their mortgages over time. The owners will likely sell the house as property values rise, if their circumstances change or if funds are needed for other priorities, like downsizing after children move out or retirement.

Ghanaians take pride in their land and home ownership as well. Yet houses are typically built in a very different manner. First, someone acquires land, whether privately or from the local chief. The person immediately builds a low wall around the space. Step by step, a foundation is laid, rebar and concrete are set and the structure is built. This often happens over a period of months or years, with additions made sporadically and often long periods of inactivity. Eventually, plumbing, electricity, the roof and windows are installed and the house is ready for the owner and family. The house is then passed down through the family.

Why such a different approach? There are many good reasons. First, Ghanaians have historically had communal ownership. The chief is responsible for holding it in trust for his people and leases it, so acquiring it involves both a traditional and legal approach. Furthermore, land tenure is often difficult to assert and enforce, so to prevent squatters or land-grabbers from claiming it, a perimeter wall establishes physical control and prevents expensive legal headaches. The next steps happen at their own pace because there is no construction company responsible for the build and banks are not able to provide mortgages at reasonable rates[12]. Thus, the owner puts their money towards the construction as it becomes available. Each contractor is engaged piecemeal and as needed, with rates negotiated every step of the way. With other competing interests (needy relatives, school fees, hospital bills, church donations), the money is not always available for Ghanaians. Slowly but surely, the house gets built and the owner will move in with the family, becoming a respected home-owning member of the community. Perhaps their funeral will be held at the house itself as a demonstration of the person's achievements.

So while the prevalent approach to home ownership is so dramatically different in Ghana, the approach is appropriate to the culture and conditions. It also can explain why foreigners who come to Ghana expecting to quickly build their home, hotel, factory or office complex quickly run into financial and logistical challenges.

---

[12] The factors leading to the current state of the Ghanaian economy are numerous, it being a product of hundreds of years of traditional practices, imposed colonial policies, unequal international trade and increasing social stratification. All of this is far too complex to address in the footnote of a guidebook, but be aware that these factors impact Ghanaians on a daily basis.

Until you understand the traits of Ghanaian culture, it will appear illogical to you. However, a greater understanding will put things like home ownership into perspective.

A Basic Cultural Profile

Per the disclaimer, culture in Ghana is complex, multifaceted and evolving, but there are commonalities that will help to explain it for outsiders.

First and foremost, Ghanaians are social. In Ghana, no man or woman is an island. In western cultures, modern life can be quite solitary: people can live lives isolated from others at home, at work and socially, desiring privacy and quiet spaces. These are rare commodities in Ghana, where large families typically live together in largely communal spaces. The expat will quickly find that people are always around, always engaging and rarely can one find a sanctuary, even in their home (especially with householp[13], gardeners and guards). Every Ghanaian they meet has networks, whether of family, friends, churchgoers, colleagues or people in the neighbourhood (e.g. vendors, tailors, chop stall owners). In an open economy where the formal legal system has limited reach, personal relations help to regulate all interactions and transactions, from getting a fair price in the market to ensuring that suppliers deliver on-time and even convincing other departments to prioritize your corporate requests. Ghanaian society and the economy are based on personal networks and observing and embracing this will be key to your success.

Ghanaians are also communal. As in many African societies, in Ghana, "a person is a person because of people"[14]. There is an

---

[13] "Househelp" is the locally-accepted term for a domestic worker. The term is commonly used in Ghana, but in other cultures and contexts can be considered outdated or offensive.

underlying concept of equity to social relations and sharing is essential, whether helping extended family members in need, or providing appropriate hospitality for a guest. In a country where large families are the norm and many live in poverty, Ghanaians make decisions not only on their self-interest, but in the interest of their family and friends[15]. For family breadwinners working in offices, this affects their daily decision-making. Whether or not you agree with this idea, as an expat with means and money, you will be expected to contribute your fair share, whether through preferential hiring, gift-giving, supporting friends in need or paying an inflated price at the market.

Ghanaians are harmonious. Everyday life in Ghana, particularly in the cities, seems chaotic: traffic[16], street vendors, yelling in the streets, markets that spill onto sidewalks and improvised or half-built structures. Look beyond this and you will see an order to things. Ghanaians favour harmony in social relations, which extends to business relations and office politics, leading to many unwritten rules and norms that maintain this balance. For example, it may be an employee's "turn" to take on a desirable task like a business trip, even if the manager believes that another person would be more effective. Ensuring harmony can explain the need in Ghana for formal meetings and events with specific protocols to observe. It also explains why rituals have such importance in Ghana, from the mundane (the requirement for formal greetings) to the special (outdoorings, weddings and funerals). Some Ghanaians will go to extreme lengths to avoid conflict, minimize differences, and do things covertly or with ulterior purposes – even veering into the supernatural. It also can make personnel management challenging, as

---

[14] This proverb is commonly known as Ubuntu.
[15] Inversely, one Ghanaian noted that self-interest can drive this, since scratching one's back means yours may be scratched.
[16] One expat commented: "Traffic in Ghana is kinda like jazz. You're all moving to your own beat, improvising, trying new things. And somehow it works."

there can be a hidden layer to office politics, including hiring and firing employees. This can be frustrating, but a crucial unwritten rule is to never lose your cool, as one who demonstrates anger (even when justified) breaks the harmony and will lose the respect of their peers.

Ghanaians are also tangential. This is a very subtle trait that takes time for outsiders to understand. Ghanaians will often speak in ways that are considered by foreigners to be roundabout or irrelevant, or even dishonest. However, it is often to avoid giving offense, disrespect or disappointment. In particular, it is taboo in Ghana to provide bad news[17]. This happens primarily to maintain harmony, but it can be challenging for an expat to comprehend. How does a leader manage an organization without knowing the depth of its challenges or receiving critical feedback? Thus, it is important to understand the subtext and read between the lines. It is also important to build trust with colleagues and learn how to ask them probing questions in the correct manner. Ghanaians will often tell you things in the abstract, answering questions with questions, or even using stories, proverbs and parables, which will have a specific point, but it is up to you as the listener to discern what is being said[18].

You will also need to choose your words carefully, as there is a fine art to providing constructive criticism and bad news to Ghanaians.

Ghanaians are proud. There is personal, family, community and national pride[19], all of which forms the core of one's personal

---

[17] For example, if a Ghanaian is abroad and her aunt has died, a relation will not call to say this, but rather, "Your auntie is unwell and she has asked for you to come home." The message is coded, but the response is clear: go now, because something terrible has happened.

[18] To underline this indirect style, an Akan proverb goes: "The wise are spoken to in proverbs, not plain language."

[19] A brief look at Ghana's rich history points to the sources of such pride: the Ashanti Empire was a powerful kingdom that conquered most of what is now Ghana and was only conquered by the British Empire after almost 80 years of wars. Ghana became the first Sub-Saharan colony to achieve independence and was for years a

identity, particularly for Ghanaian men. An outward sign of this is the way in which Ghanaians dress in public: men take care in their appearance and favour stylish business clothing and closely-cropped hair, while women wear stunning dresses and smart business wear, always with impeccably-coiffed hair. Injuring another's pride in Ghana is a serious offense, whether by real or perceived slights. Consequently, expats should take care to avoid direct insults, but also to learn the taboos and faux-pas that can offend Ghanaians. On the other hand, playing to another's sense of pride can be a savvy business move.

Ghanaians are also hierarchical. In a twist on communal thinking, an Akan proverb reads "someone sits on someone else." In contrast to cultures that value equality and flat social structures, Ghanaian society has historically been hierarchical, starting in the household and extending to the village, clan and kingdom[20]. Decisions were made by the leaders and the rest were expected to follow. This trend continues, as elders are given respect and men are assumed to play primary decision-making roles. The education system, informed by British-style rote learning and Ghanaian deference to authority, reinforces hierarchical behaviours and aversion to speaking out of turn. Ghana's unequal development has stratified society further, exacerbating this phenomenon. As a consequence, Ghanaians are highly sensitive to hierarchy and their place within it. For example, when a meeting or event includes an important "Big Man/Woman", it can be delayed for hours until the guest of honour arrives. Expats typically come in high on the social ladder, but are often blissfully unaware of their place. Expats may find themselves addressed as

---

leader in the independence and pan-African movements. It still leads or is otherwise influential in many sectors (e.g. diplomacy, football and music) and is the regional hub for many international organizations in West Africa. While Ghana faces many challenges, it occupies an outsized role in Africa and seeks to be a global leader.

[20] There is a communal twist to this: in most traditional societies in Ghana, the chief is a first among equals and makes decisions in discussion with other elders. This style of leadership in the workplace will be explored later.

boss, master, madam, sir, mummy, daddy, auntie, or *uncle*, which can be uncomfortable, but with some understanding and practice, they will be dishing out these everyday honorifics as well. Female expats may find themselves having to work harder to earn the default respect accorded to their male peers and males may need to gently but firmly ensure that female peers are recognized and included.

Ghanaians are spiritual. Since time immemorial, Ghana has been a spiritual place. This continues in modern society, whether in the village or in Accra. For Ghanaians, nothing is attributed to chance, but to forces beyond their control, often by God, but for many also by gods, ancestors and other spirits, who play a role in day-to-day affairs. Because of this, Ghanaians assume that whatever one's personal circumstances, God is always in control[21]. Even death is to be welcomed: it is a sad event for the living, but a call to glory for the deceased. For the foreigner, modern science and technology operate alongside a spirituality that can sometimes enter the work realm.

Ghanaians are also religious. How does one give thanks to God or to the gods? Through one's religion. Almost every Ghanaian has a religious affiliation, whether Christian, Muslim or animist. Foreigners will see this immediately: from billboards for glittering mega-churches led by celebrity pastors to the ubiquitous *trotro* minibuses proclaiming the greatness of Allah. On Sunday mornings, the roads and shops are deserted and those living near a mosque will be able to tell the time of day from the call to prayer. For Ghanaians, churches and mosques are social hubs for networking, entertainment and social services – so worship is only one small part of the equation. Religion in Ghana is not limited to the place of worship or

---

[21] A popular bumper sticker declares the vehicle "covered by the blood of Jesus". On a more lighthearted note, someone who is naturally bald can say, "The Lord is my barber". Kponor, Michael. *Ghana's Best Guide to Pidgin English.* Global Mamas, Accra. 2012. P. 24.

the home but also the place of work. Offices may features posters with praise to God, e-mail signature blocks may feature religious proverbs and a colleague's cellphone ringtone may be a praise and worship song. Even government meetings will begin and end with a prayer – typically one Christian, one Muslim. Religious tolerance in Ghana is very high but foreigners who are not used to discussing their personal beliefs may find it uncomfortable to address the subject, including divulging to others their beliefs (or non-beliefs, in the case of agnostics and atheists).

Interestingly, animism still colours the lives of many Christians and Muslims who hold a Bible or Qur'an in one hand and worship their ancestors with the other. Spiritualist healers seek to provide supernatural cures to ailments and fetish priests can use *juju* to place a curse on an enemy. "Witchcraft" is also widely believed to be the cause of many problems, which often marginalizes women. This religious pluralism is complex, but makes sense based on other traits in the Ghanaian cultural profile[22]. These beliefs can collide with modern office politics, when disagreements between Ghanaian colleagues or business problems can lead to accusations of witchcraft and other spiritually-related issues. Indeed, the foreigner may find that their "irrational" is rational in Ghana and may need to understand these better to deal effectively with them.

Together, these cultural traits help to explain Ghanaian culture and to explain the rationale behind behaviours that can confuse and frustrate foreigners, particularly in the office. Throughout the book, these will appear both explicitly and implicitly.

---

[22] It also can be comparable to other spiritual beliefs in other cultures that manifest themselves. The Catholic and Anglican churches recognize the power of saints to intercede on behalf of the living. Cultures also see luck and bad luck through numbers. For example, a building may not have a 13th floor due to its connotation of bad luck in the West, while the same thing happens regarding the number 4 in China.

Other Important Cultural Attitudes

In addition, there are other traits that are very common within Ghanaian culture. These may have significant effects on how you work with Ghanaians.

Gender Roles

Attitudes to gender relations are traditional in Ghana and women and men are implicitly assumed to have their place in the hierarchy. At the household level, men have been the official heads of the family and the primary breadwinners. Men take pride in their families and in their ability to provide. At the community and societal level, men have historically been expected to make the decisions.

However, after a short time in Ghana, a foreigner will notice many single mothers running successful businesses while managing the household and raising children. Indeed, women in Ghana take on a "triple-burden" of paid work, unpaid housework and community involvement. Their hard work often goes unnoticed in Ghana, but foreigners have taken note, as many tend to favour hiring women over men for their perceived integrity and work ethic and to avoid "old boys" networks.

There is a great deal of lip service to gender equality in Ghana, yet so little gender equality in practice. This is particularly the case in leadership positions: women make up only 40 of 270 parliamentarians[23] and 8 of 40 cabinet and regional ministers[24].

---

[23] Source: https://citinewsroom.com/2021/01/women-representation-in-ghanas-parliaments-infographic/
[24] Source: https://www.presidency.gov.gh/index.php/briefing-room/press-releases/1854-president-akufo-addo-s-new-government

Female CEOs are rare. Meetings in all sectors seem to be overwhelmingly male and the women in the room are often there to take notes or bring tea and snacks to the participants.

Patriarchal attitudes have persisted and maintained this status quo, in spite of efforts to level the playing field in the office. These attitudes have ramifications outside the office as well: the Ghanaian version of machismo can lead to an expectation that a mistress is acceptable (or necessary) and many Big Men with wealth and power walk a fine line between being an upstanding and religious family man while being the sugar daddy who takes care of his woman (or women) on the side[25]. Women are too often expected to be subservient to both their husbands and their lovers.

Yet for all of these challenges, Ghanaian women have held important positions of power, including royal (Ashanti war leader Yaa Asantewaa) and legal (two recent Supreme Court chief justices). Ghanaian women will demonstrate their prowess when the opportunity is there. Sometimes that requires opening the door and insisting that they walk through it – while ensuring that the men get out of the way. Regardless, foreigners routinely declare hiring Ghanaian women a smart, if not superior, choice.

Foreign women seem to be accorded more respect and deference, but will experience these attitudes and will need to navigate through these[26]. At the street level, some men (particularly those with no experience interacting with foreign women) may feel the right to call at you or touch you or casually propose marriage. Brush off these quickly, as these behaviours are not accepted by Ghanaian women. In the office and in formal situations, this sexism will be more subtle.

---

[25] Male foreigners have also reported a pressure to take on a mistress by male Ghanaian colleagues.
[26] As non-Ghanaians, foreign women are sometimes seen as a third sex. Regardless, patriarchal attitudes will still be experienced regularly.

So foreign women will need to assert themselves quickly and regularly. However, they can also be effective examples and mentors of their female Ghanaian peers and employees.

Foreign men also have a role to play in shaping gender relations, particularly if they occupy a place in the hierarchy. Men can display positive norms of masculinity and use their decision-making power to hire strong and competent women, promote equitable human resource policies (like leave provisions) and ensure that female colleagues and employees have the opportunity and space to manage and lead in planning, meetings and operations[27].

Short-Term vs Long-Term Thinking

Foreigners find that short-term thinking seems to predominate life in Ghana. Indeed, the challenges of daily life in Ghana often require a focus on short-term needs, including dealing with daily crises and placating the demands of others, which feeds into maintaining social harmony. This is observed in small businesses and government bureaucracies. However, remember the description above of how a house is built: it appears to be a series of short-term decisions, but over time, they lead towards a longer-term goal.

These challenges are common in any workplace, but may seem more prevalent in Ghana. In your work, you may find that you will need to ensure that your colleagues and employees understand the longer-term goals of the organization. Then you can use this awareness to orient their work towards achieving these goals and to avoid focusing on the day-to-day crises that can distract. If an employee is working on something outside of the organizational plan, ask what the ultimate goal is and how they plan to achieve this[28].

---

[27] Research organizations like Promundo have resources on how men can contribute positively to gender equality. https://promundoglobal.org/

Accra vs Everywhere Else

Most foreigners coming to Ghana live and work in Accra. The city is a booming, bulging, sprawling mix of glittering office towers, concrete government offices, and ramshackle kiosks. It also has perhaps the most developed infrastructure in the country, even if electricity is unreliable, roads seem to be choked with traffic and sidewalks are sporadic, filled with vendors and missing the occasional brick.

For Ghanaians, Accra is where things happen, the place of opportunity. The bright lights of the big city attract people from all walks of life, from students to entrepreneurs to bureaucrats to villagers employed in manual labour and *kayayei*[29]. It also is an expensive city for Ghanaians and without a healthy income, staying afloat requires daily perseverance. Ghanaians use their social networks with family and friends to get a foothold in the city and to keep their costs low. The elevated costs of living in Accra (from housing to transport) require this and visitors do not stay long. Accra also seems to be constantly growing, so affordable housing may lie up to two hours away from the office.

Accra may be *the* big city, but it is not the only one: nearby, the deepwater port of Tema feeds the capital and much of the country with imported goods. Further inland, Kumasi is the central hub. Without embassies and government offices to support it, Kumasi relies on business to sustain its prosperity, which are overwhelmingly Ghanaian. Takoradi has historically been Ghana's third city economically, having its own deepwater port and rail

---

[28] This will be discussed further in in Managing and Leading Ghanaians

[29] Kayayei refers mostly to women and girls selling goods at traffic stops; this is some of the hardest, most precarious and dangerous work in Ghana. Many women and girls from rural and remote areas end up as kayayei in Accra.

access to the interior bauxite and gold mines. This easygoing fishing town surrounded by beaches recently has been the central point for offshore oil drilling and the boom has turned it into a sort of Wild West. In the North, Tamale is the main city. It seems to be sleepy, but is also a lively place of trading and a hub for agricultural goods from Northern Ghana and surrounding countries[30].

In all of these places, there are opportunities for business, but there are also more deeply-entrenched systems, networks, cultural practices and ways of doing things that have persisted for longer periods of time. Operating in any of these requires a good analysis before jumping in, as what works in Accra[31] may not work in Tamale and what works in Takoradi may not work in Kumasi. And what works in *any* of these places may not work in rural areas. While cities have developed quickly in recent decades, life in rural Ghana has changed very slowly and traditional ways persist.

The Hustle: Nobody Has Just One Job

Foreigners coming to Ghana are attracted by the Ghanaian entrepreneurial spirit, a reputation built on a history of trading and an openness to income-generating opportunities. However, this "Ghanaian entrepreneurial spirit" can also be understood as "Ghanaians work a lot of businesses". In discussions with Ghanaian 9-5ers, one quickly realizes that many are not simply clocking in and out and enjoying the quiet evenings, but hustling to earn extra income to support family members or compensate for an inadequate

---

[30] It is worth mentioning again that there is a major divide between Northern Ghana and Southern Ghana that is geographical, economic, cultural and religious.

[31] Foreigners are concentrated primarily in Accra as well, so people working in office towers, embassies and non-governmental organizations can quickly lose sight of the bigger picture in the country and its people, who have a much different experience. If your work involves other parts of the country, it is important to get out of Accra and understand it better.

social safety net. The office manager also works on the side in real estate; the shea butter producer also imports used clothes; the NGO project advisor runs a missionary operation; the househelp caters to weekend parties; and the lawyer is working on his run for the local constituency seat. For those without steady jobs, having multiple sources of income is even more important to make ends meet: the musician sells protein shakes; the tailor also sharpens knives; the provisions store owner charges cellphones.

Find out what your colleagues do outside of work. Chances are they will have another endeavour. It might be an issue, especially if it impacts your team's work or presents a conflict of interest, but it could also be an opportunity to expand one's network. Talk to your employees and colleagues to ensure that they fully understand the concept of a potential conflict of interest in your culture and that your organization comes first.

GMT: Ghana Maybe Time

Ghana sits on the prime meridian and observes Greenwich Mean Time. However, a common refrain among expats and Ghanaians alike is that "GMT" means something completely different: for expats, it is "Ghana Maybe Time" and for Ghanaians, "Ghana Man Time". GMT is the lived experience of time through a Ghanaian perspective. Broadly speaking, it is seen as a lack of attention and adherence to the clock and a more flexible conception of "time" itself.

This manifests itself in many ways, but expats will notice it immediately: colleagues may not show up to work on time, team meetings may begin late, official functions start late and go well beyond their official end, external meetings and appointments may not happen at all, deadlines are missed and deliveries late. GMT has roots in traditional culture, when clocks did not govern the day. However, it also has a modern function of regulating life in a way that reduces stress and allows overly-busy people to set priorities and determine what is really "important" or "urgent".

For expats, this often means a departure from their orderly understanding of how a society "should" work, based on their own culture (or the idealized version of their homeland). The gap between this unrealistic expectation and the lived experience in Ghana leads to frustration over delayed or cancelled appointments and meetings as well as unmet deadlines. The longer the delay, the more frustrated the expat, who bemoans that others do not show him/her respect and that he/she could have done something more important rather than waiting or expecting something to happen.

Unlike expats, most Ghanaians do not shop at international malls, eat at expat-owned restaurants or live in well-appointed private compounds near the office. GMT is a fact of everyday life from the moment they wake up to when they fall asleep.

Consider that the average commute for a Ghanaian to downtown Accra is between 1-2 hours using public transportation on congested roads of varying quality. If it rains, the house might have leaks to attend to and the roads may flood or wash out completely. Not to mention ensuring that children are fed, dressed and off to school under these conditions. Is it no surprise that Ghanaian colleagues might show up late to the office (or even late to an online meeting)?

GMT varies by location. In a small town or village, time is very flexible. On the other extreme, embassies and high commissions operate as small oases of international standard time.

There are a few tricks that can mitigate the effect of GMT:

1) If you can't predict what will happen: Find ways to optimize your time. If you are worried about potentially wasted time while you wait for a meeting or appointment, bring a document you need to review or a report you have been meaning to read (but have never had the time to do it). Ensure that your smartphone has a charge and that you can conduct business, but try to avoid unproductive and aimless internet usage.

2) If you can predict what will happen: Try to adjust accordingly. Before setting a meeting, think strategically. Set your watch to GMT: if you have colleagues who you know will be 30 minutes late, set it officially at 9:00AM, but set your own calendar for 9:30. If you are meeting with a Big Man/Woman, like an executive or government minister, reschedule your other appointments rather than stressing over whether you will make your next engagement. Try an appointment for early in the day, before competing priorities and further delays can occur.

3) If it is a problem in your own office: discuss with your colleagues. Ask them what they think of your idea of punctuality and their own. If your colleagues are habitually late, ask what is causing this. You will be able to better understand your colleagues and feel less frustrated when you understand their perspectives. In turn, you can share your country and/or company's cultural perspective on punctuality to help your colleagues understand why it is important and to earn their respect and support for your ideas. If you can approach this in a non-judgemental and pragmatic manner, your proposed remedies are more likely to be received and owned by the team.

4) If you have the ability to change things: find solutions for your team. Ghanaians often feel frustrated by GMT as well, so it could be a starting point for making positive changes collaboratively. For example: if team members jointly set meeting times, they are more likely to take ownership and responsibility and times are more likely to be realistic. If a meeting is to start on time, start with the most important items first so that the absentees are indirectly penalized and not the attendees.

Results will vary, but remember to work within your own personal and professional sphere of influence. You may be able to foster a workplace environment without GMT, but it could cost you your sanity, so choose your battles wisely.

Cultural Rituals: Weddings, Outdoorings and Funerals

Every culture celebrates the milestones of life and in Ghana, these take on their own forms, informed by ethnic and religious traditions. The fervor with which Ghanaians celebrate these can have an impact on your office environment, your weekend schedule and your wallet.

An outdooring is a ceremony in which a newborn child is introduced to the community by the family and receives its name[32]. This typically occurs eight days after birth.

A Ghanaian wedding was once a simple informal ceremony between a man, woman and their community; over time it has expanded to something much larger. For those who can afford it, weddings involve two parts: First is the smaller traditional ceremony, which happens in the home village. The second is the larger "modern" ceremony: it is held in a church, the bride wears a white dress and the groom a suit and food and drink are served. As in western

---

[32] There are often rules for this. For Akans, babies often receive a Christian name, but also their traditional names based on the day of the week, their birth order and other notable characteristics.
Example 1: John Evans Fiifi Atta Mills was a Christian (John Evans), Friday-born Fante male (Fiifi) and a twin (Atta).
Example 2: Someone who is a Friday-born Ashanti male, born a twin and fourth-oldest child takes the name of *Kofi Atta Annan*, the name of the former United Nations Secretary-General.

culture, wedding ceremonies have recently seen an increase in size and complexity, leading to a very high cost for young Ghanaians.

Funerals have seen a massive increase in prominence in recent years. When a Ghanaian dies, there is a series of events depending on the particular culture and status of the dead. For better or for worse, funerals are now expensive, multiple-day affairs[33] and are part of the Ghanaian social calendar.

In most cases, it will not happen immediately: funerals require the raising of significant sums of money for mortuary fees, catering costs, entertainment and decorations[34]. Social media aside, word still travels slowly in Ghana: advertisements are not only printed in newspapers, but colourful posters are posted on walls and even the backs of trotros to get the word out. Consequently, funerals often take place a month after the actual death.

Attending a funeral can be a major commitment. Saturdays are for funeral rites and Sundays for thanksgiving services. If a funeral is in a distant village, it could require travel on Friday and/or Monday. This leads to a lot of long weekends for Ghanaian workers.

There is a high social desirability to going to weddings and especially funerals for Ghanaians. In the end, if you do not attend the weddings and funerals of others, who will come to yours? These ceremonies are also important for networking. Big Men and Women are there to be seen, as business can be conducted on the margins.

For all three ceremonies, you may find yourself invited by colleagues. The main question for a foreigner to ask is: what is

---

[33] There are two exceptions to this: Muslims typically bury their dead within 48 hours and Mormons are known in Ghana for having modest funerals.
[34] Elisabeth Ohene wryly observed, "If you see a house being painted anywhere in Ghana, you can safely assume that someone has died and that there is a funeral coming up in that house." http://www.bbc.com/news/world-africa-26838635

expected of me? The best first step is to ask trusted Ghanaian colleagues for advice.

Often, your physical presence is desired, but not required. As a leader, your attendance brings honour to the hosts (or deceased). When travel and time is a major consideration, you can attend a part of the ceremony – at least stay to accept food – and then leave early. When done tactfully, it will be understood and accepted.

If a colleague passes away or a close family member passes (parents, children), you will be expected to attend, unless informed otherwise. If a member of the extended family, it may be best for another colleague to attend on the office's behalf.

More important is the financial expectation: weddings and funerals are expensive affairs. Consequently, Ghanaians do not typically accept a card and flowers – send money. Whatever amount is contributed will be appreciated[35]. Find out if your office has a social welfare fund, by which colleagues contribute to a common pot and provide support when needed. If not, when tragedy strikes, expect that colleagues will pass the hat for contributions.

If attending, inquire about proper dress, particularly with funerals: for a sudden or early death, mourners will wear black and red; for the death of a prosperous or elderly person, black and white. In both instances, there is particular cloth that can be purchased in the market, so call up your tailor or seamstress[36].

Regardless of the politics around them, outdoorings, weddings and funerals are major cultural events that give insight into Ghanaian culture, so you should strive to attend at least one of each.

---

[35] A foreigner might feel the urge to note that a funeral, the money might have been better spent on the living's hospital fees, but it is best not to comment on this.

[36] As with househelp, the traditionally-minded labels still apply in Ghana.

Property and Ownership

The concept of property is quite fluid in Ghana, where social networks mean that so many things are held communally and that one cannot lay claim to being the sole owner of something. Land is a prime example: one can own land in Ghana, but this depends greatly on the circumstances. Some land is owned privately outright with a government deed. Or one may have land that was passed down through the family, but based on an informal arrangement which could discourage long-term planning. And if someone has built on your land, getting them off it will be a massive headache, even if you can demonstrate ownership with legal documents (which is not always possible). For this reason, when someone acquires land, the first thing they often do is build a low wall, simply to demonstrate a physical claim to a space. Outsiders from British colonizers to the World Bank have tried to standardize property in a pro-Western fashion to promote economic activity, with varying results.

In most areas, land is held communally. In this case, if someone wishes to use land for housing, farming or business, they must formally ask permission of the chief. As the traditional ruler, the chief nominally owns the land, but in reality administers it for the good of the people. This land can be leased privately for up to 99 years but can never be owned. Ownership issues can get complex, as anyone in the mining industry can confirm.

Communal ownership and responsibility reaches to the most personal levels. In a village, one has parents and one may have children, but aunts, uncles and additional wives have an important role in their development and can take the place of their birth parents when required. So if you asked in a village who are a person's children, it would be rude, as they are in a sense *all* their children.

Thus property in Ghana is a mix of communal and hierarchical politics at play. If you are a foreigner owning or managing an operation with a relatively substantial budget and employ Ghanaians with relatively little means, the organization's resources may be seen as communal goods held in trust by the leader (i.e. you) and used for unintended purposes.

Offices around the world face the challenge of misuse of supplies, but when a printer or a vehicle is a luxury and the opportunity is there, the chance of misuse can increase. Consequently, you may need to pay special attention and track the usage of goods. For example, vehicles may need fuel and usage logbooks to ensure that they are not used as personal transport for a weekend funeral[37].

Service

Customer relations in Ghana are quite different than in western countries. In Ghana, the customer is *not* always right[38]. Indeed, some expats may leave a business feeling that they did a disservice to the server! Rather than wait to be eagerly served, you may need to get the attention of a server to meet your needs. The server will tell you "Please, it's coming", which does mean that it is coming at some point in the future – but that could be in one minute or one hour. You might also find that your server seems to be neglecting your needs, while discouraging other servers from interacting with you, who they will see as rightfully "their customer".

Ghanaian customers tend to be quite forward and brusque: at restaurants it is common to hear a patron order "bring me this" and offer sharp criticism – all without making eye contact with the

---

[37] This will be discussed further in Managing and Leading Ghanaians.

[38] Unless the customer is a Big Man/Woman.

server. In the hierarchy, the customer or patron is being served and must make it clear that they expect the service.

This may or may not work well for you. Expats as customers in Ghana need to blend politeness and friendliness but also an assertiveness. This allows the person to be respectful, while also not being taken for granted by the server / sales associate / customer service representative. This requires a lot of tact and patience, particularly when using government services (especially since there's no competition). A neglected customer can quickly become a frustrated and angry customer, but remember that in a harmonious Ghanaian culture, when you lose your cool, you lose the respect of others.

However, customer relations are highly valued for market sellers. Once you have purchased from a seller, they will expect to see you again and will be jealous of any competition, seeing you as "their customer". Other sellers may recognize this norm and you approaching them for business directly may get awkward, even if the price is better.

So choose your produce vendor wisely, especially if in a small town. To keep a regular customer happy, a seller of produce should provide their freshest goods and may "dash" their customer an extra mango or bananas as a symbol of gratitude for their patronage and symbol of friendship. If you do not receive a dash, you should reconsider your choice of vendor[39]!

If you employ Ghanaians providing a service, you may need to work with them to explain the standards that you seek to set and to instill the desired service mentality[40].

---

[39] This will be discussed further in Negotiation.
[40] Specific examples by occupation are provided in Annex: Working With...

Maintenance

Ghanaians themselves will tell you that there is not much of a "maintenance culture" in Ghana. Things tend to work until they do not, then they get fixed, replaced, or done without. A classic example is a vehicle: when an expat hears a strange noise while driving, the instinct is to investigate it quickly, as it could end up being more trouble if the problem worsens or the vehicle breaks down entirely. For the average Ghanaian, vehicles are expensive and maintenance eats into the bottom line. So when a car produces a strange noise, one takes note, but why spend money on something that *might* become a problem in the future? When it breaks, *then* it is a problem[41].

However, western countries can easily be accused of not having a maintenance culture. When a computer or household appliance malfunctions, one can simply throw it away and buy a new one. Ghanaians almost always keep or pass on things of value. A cellphone with a broken screen is still a working cellphone, a broken door handle on a truck can always be tied down and a dustpan with a broken handle can (with effort) still receive dust. So while things are often not maintained to a western standard in Ghana, they are used as long as they continue to function. Again, it is not a problem until it is definitively broken and unusable[42].

Regardless, when running an organization, maintenance is an important consideration, whether it be for buildings, vehicles, office furniture or products. If you have employees responsible for

---

[41] This general perception leads to interesting behaviour. Namely, expat-owned cars are sold on the market at a premium, as buyers assume that they have been maintained better by their foreign owners (which may be true or not!).

[42] Likewise, there is a recycling culture in Ghana: non-functioning items often find second lives. Electronics and appliances are left on doorsteps and taken by informal scrap collectors to be broken down and the valuable parts taken. So while waste is a massive issue and formal recycling only happens with select items (mostly bottles, which have deposit value), there is certainly a recycling culture.

maintenance, ensure that they fully understand the organization's requirements.

Cultural Translators

This is not an exhaustive nor definitive list of traits of the Ghanaian cultural profile. You may experience these in different ways or find that they are not applicable to your case at all. Understanding Ghanaian culture is a continuous journey and it requires regular analysis and the ability to ask questions. You will rely on colleagues or people in your network to help understand patterns of behaviour in Ghana – but make sure that you build a rapport with Ghanaian colleagues in whom you can confide to help you along the way. You may also wish to identify colleagues in the office who can assist as your "cultural translators" who can give you quick feedback on ideas and their appropriateness. For example, after-work drinks is a common practice in many cultures, but if your office includes people who commute long distances, people with familial obligations (a burden routinely placed on women) or people who abstain from alcohol for religious reasons, then perhaps your cultural translator would recommend a team lunch at a nearby establishment. As noted earlier, the funeral is another area where a cultural translator would be particularly helpful.

Cultural misunderstandings and faux pas are part of the journey, so do not stress too much – Ghanaians are social and harmonious and will work to extend this generosity your way. If you keep an open and analytical mind, you will be able to orient yourself as an interculturally effective person in Ghana. But what do Ghanaians think of foreigners anyway and how will this affect your work with them? The next section will explore this.

Working with Ghanaians

If you don't let your friend cross and reach (his destination), you will also not cross and reach yours.
-Ashanti proverb

Working with Ghanaians

How Ghanaians Understand Foreigners

As they disembark the plane in Accra, visitors will immediately experience the equatorial heat and humidity as they disembark the plane, but also the warm and welcoming ways of Ghanaians[43]. Indeed, Ghanaians regularly rate at the top of lists of the friendliest people in Africa[44]. Ghanaians, being social, communal and harmonious, are also welcoming and hospitable towards visitors. Guests are always welcome in the house and a meal is always offered to be shared. Someone who needs help on the street will find several people immediately pitching in to help carry a heavy load, to fix a broken car, or to provide directions – even as far as accompanying the person to their destination.

Ghanaians overall are highly welcoming of foreigners. In addition to a social and harmonious culture, Ghana has had over five hundred years of sustained contact with foreigners (for better and worse). Unlike other African countries, Ghana has not experienced major strife and has almost always been "open for business" in one form or another to foreigners. Consequently, for decades, organizations from around the world have sent their people to Ghana and Ghanaians have welcomed them from the capital down to the village[45]. In addition, many Ghanaians travel for business and higher education and know themselves what it is like to be a foreigner.

---

[43] Customs officers notwithstanding.

[44] As the Bradt Guide notes, "Ghana has a reputation as the friendliest country in West Africa, a title that is patently absurd but certainly not unjustified." P. 91

[45] An exception is when a foreigner is brought in to do work that a Ghanaian could clearly do as effectively.

Working with Ghanaians

Regardless, foreigners will immediately know that they are foreign. Ghanaian society has a diverse set of peoples, but is still mostly homogeneous. Consequently, wherever you travel in Ghana, you will be addressed on the street by your skin colour. In each language, there is an indigenous word for foreigner: In Twi, it is *obruni*, in Dagbani, it is *salaminga* and in Ewe, it is *yavoo*. Do not take this personally – you are simply being acknowledged by the way that people can immediately distinguish you[46] from locals. European, Middle Eastern and Asian people easily stand out amongst indigenous Ghanaians. While one can "fit in" by embracing Ghanaian cultural norms, food and clothing, it is near-impossible to truly "blend in". Understanding and accepting this is a major hurdle for foreigners. Even Ghanaian-born Indians and Lebanese, while part of Ghanaian society, are a step apart from most Ghanaians. Regardless, one could and should try to fit in as best they can and to transcend the obruni stereotype by integrating into Ghanaian culture. One of the best compliments one can receive is, "Oh, you are a Ghanaian!"

Foreigners with darker skin tones will be surprised on arrival to be called an obruni. This is quite simply because anyone who is not a Ghanaian is a foreigner. There is a complex difference between Ghanaians and those from other cultures who claim Ghanaian and African descent, who typically have a better integration experience, but do not automatically transcend the gap of time and space. Consequently, coming to Ghana can feel like a homecoming, but one is not always welcomed as a brother or sister[47] as many have

---

[46] For people coming from cultures with racial conflict or a history of racism, calling someone by the colour of their skin or their immigration status would be highly taboo. Remember that in spite of the history in Ghana of the slave trade and colonialism, the personal experience of racism for most Ghanaians is fundamentally different from those of other cultures. Case in point: obruni means "person from beyond the seas" and yavoo "tricky dog", as noted by Stephen Atta Owusu. https://www.primenewsghana.com/general-news/why-akans-gas-ewes-and-northerners-get-called-pepeni-eblutorwo-ayigbefuo-and-senu.html

discovered. Some have left the country quite disillusioned. However, Ghana becomes more globally connected, attitudes are changing. Even the government has seized on this with its highly successful *Year of Return, Ghana 2019* campaign. Yet for whomever chooses to move to Ghana, they will need to face the challenges of expensive groceries, unreliable electricity and internet, an unhelpful bureaucracy and a complex society and working culture. As Ghanaian-American M.anifest raps: there's no shortcut to heaven. In spite of these challenges, immigrants from the diaspora and professionals who have returned to Ghana from abroad report enjoying work and live in a culture that gives them space to be entrepreneurs and without the overt racism that impedes their social and professional lives elsewhere. There are returnee and expat professional communities to provide support and a growing literature of experience upon which one can draw[48].

Ghanaians are more ambivalent about other Africans. During Africa's struggle for independence, the young nation of Ghana was a hotbed of revolutionary activity and thinking, hosting future leaders from across the continent and actively promoting unity and pan-Africanism. Ghana holds an important place in African society and Ghanaians are proud of its history, yet these links have not been maintained and so the average Ghanaian has fairly limited knowledge of other African countries. Ghanaians and their Franco-West African cousins (including immediate neighbours Cote

---

[47] For many Ghanaians seeking to immigrate to western countries, they might question why someone would leave it all to move to Ghana. For example, the American-born Imakus Njinga Okofu Ababio and Nana Okofo spent decades petitioning the Government of Ghana to be granted Ghanaian citizenship.

[48] These often don't mince words. Consider reading Jemila Abdulai's "Returning to Ghana? My Returnee Story and What You Need to Know" (https://circumspecte.com/2019/08/returning-to-ghana-returnee-story-jemila-abdulai/) and Paul Boakye's "What Nobody Tells You About Moving to Ghana as an African-American or Caribbean Returnee" (https://writeonline.medium.com/7-things-nobody-tells-you-about-moving-to-ghana-355bf9e76283).

d'Ivoire, Burkina Faso and Togo) do not intermingle unless they have a common family and ethnic group. South Africans are known primarily through their businesses that are expanding throughout Accra and its shopping malls. Africans from other countries thus occupy a space somewhere between local and foreigner.

However, Ghanaians *definitely* have opinions on Nigerians, who are highly prevalent, particularly in Accra, but also secondary cities. In contrast to the harmonious and tangential Ghanaians, Nigerians are perceived by Ghanaians as being direct, pushy and not always trustworthy[49]. Nigerians are also blamed for all sorts of criminality, particularly when the culprit is not known. (On the other hand, in Nigeria, Ghanaian immigrants have historically been blamed for the country's economic woes.) Regardless, Nigerians can be found in the upper echelons of businesses, at universities, as traders and as property owners. Ghanaians are also voracious consumers of Nigeria's massive "Nollywood" film industry and pop music. Ghanaians and Nigerians also enjoy a friendly cultural rivalry over who has the superior recipe for jollof rice.

Regardless of these challenges, Ghanaians are highly welcoming of foreigners. But how a foreigner is perceived by Ghanaians depends in part on the reason why they came. Foreigners from outside of West Africa are mostly perceived as privileged: they have jobs, disposable incomes, they have passports and if things get difficult, they have return tickets home.

For people with little means or income, foreigners could be a potential employer or buyer of services. Ghanaians are communal and help each other, so as a privileged person, you will be expected to do your share. This can be quite challenging to navigate if you

---

[49] Given that Nigerians are typically economic migrants without a social safety net, Ghanaians probably encounter the most entrepreneurial ones who need to work the hardest to prosper in a foreign land.

come from an individualistic society, particularly where asking for money and favours is a serious matter or even taboo. However, integrating into Ghanaian culture without embracing this communal spirit can be particularly challenging.

Businesspeople

For the first few decades since independence in 1957, it seemed that foreigners were mostly either diplomats in the capital and volunteers elsewhere, with a few multinational representatives and entrepreneurs sprinkled in. Regardless, business and trade have always been part of the local economy. In recent years, Ghana's economic growth has attracted the international business community, with international companies looking to establish a foothold in the Ghanaian and regional economy and entrepreneurs looking to strike it rich with hotels, restaurants and consulting and logistical services. In particular, after the discovery of drillable oil in 2008, the economy heated up and foreigners flocked to get a piece of the action. The economy cooled off, but most of the foreigners remained. Those who have stayed have often continued doing business, buying property, starting families and have integrated into society to varying degrees.

Diplomats

Diplomats are ubiquitous in Accra, which hosts a long list of foreign embassies (including United Nations offices) and diplomats. Diplomats are accorded significant respect in Ghana, both in their privileges (avoiding the wrath of police and exemptions from taxes) and in what they are believed to bring to Ghana: technical expertise, trade opportunities, funding for development projects and disposable incomes. Whether they accept it or not, diplomats are part of the economic top 1% of Ghanaian society: They live in the nicest houses downtown, have large vehicles and employ guards, househelp, drivers and gardeners. They fly around the world, take regular vacations, shop at supermarkets, eat at restaurants and get waved through police roadblocks. Aware of this privilege, diplomats can make friends with Ghanaians, but are also wary that some see them as a source of opportunity. In particular, diplomats are also assumed to know shortcuts to getting a visa. As a result, diplomats can be mistrustful of Ghanaians and questioning of their intentions. Some of this concern is valid, but it can also lead diplomats to live isolated lives and prevent them from making friends and fostering deeper relationships with Ghanaians and can be a large missed opportunity, especially as their stays in Ghana last only a few years.

Development Workers

Non-governmental organizations (NGOs) and their workers are found throughout Ghana. From international NGOs with national and regional programming based in Accra to smaller organizations working in towns and communities, to informal organizations at the village level. Foreigners working for NGOs in Ghana are generally welcomed as people with experience in their field who have come to make a positive contribution as well as bring financial resources.

There is a wide spectrum of NGO workers from salaried employees of an organization and those who are unpaid volunteers. The former can have long-term contracts, housing and accompanying families (like diplomats), while the latter can be short-term and highly budget-conscious, living in homestays, eating chop and taking trotros. Ghanaians may not distinguish between the two, as NGOs proliferate the country and seem to undertake all sorts of work. So explaining who you are and what you are in Ghana to do in a short "elevator pitch" speech can be helpful anywhere.

Working with Ghanaians

Development work is a major industry, providing money, jobs and other resources in places that have missed out on economic opportunities or have been neglected by the government. Money talks in Ghana and people will be interested if you are bringing something to the table – and disappointed when they find out if you seemed to but did not. When meeting with government officials or community leaders, you may wish to clarify whether or not you bring financial resources to your project, who will be responsible for it and when it will be happening. Development projects typically have a public launch event, which can raise expectations of all sorts of stakeholders.

There is also a very long history of development projects in Ghana, some of which have been successful and many of which have not; Ghanaians will be able to quickly judge whether yours will be worth supporting. However, you may not fully understand the actual level of support, as tangential behaviour will not immediately reveal whether your warm welcome and public celebration will be backed by genuine support and confidence in the project. This will require a critical analysis and probing questions of stakeholders to determine what people really think of your work[50].

Missionaries

Throughout Ghana's contact with foreigners, Islamic and Christian missionaries have been prevalent, leading to the current religious makeup of the country. Ghanaians are highly spiritual and there is a great deal of religious exchange[51].

---

[50] If significant resources are involved, a community may not be able to refuse, even if the plan is not feasible. An example later will demonstrate this.

[51] This exchange works both ways: with foreigners coming to Ghana as missionaries and Ghanaians fervently spreading the Word of God in evangelical megachurches and Catholic parishes in Anglophone countries.

While a casual observer would think that Ghanaians are more religious than other nations, there still appears to be room for missionaries. For example, the Jesus Christ Church of Latter-Day Saints (or Mormonism) sends local and foreign missionaries for door-to-door evangelization across the country. Religious organizations also have significant spiritual and charitable operations and themselves are very involved in grassroots development work.

Missionaries may receive the warmest welcome of all of foreigners as they seek to connect with Ghanaians on a personal and spiritual level. Most Ghanaians may not understand the mission of a technical advisor supporting a governance project or a tourist taking trotros to see ancient rock formations, but Muslims and Christians alike can appreciate the mission of an evangelist.

Tourists

Tourism in Ghana is relatively modest, but significant. Ghanaians see travellers curiously, as travel for Ghanaians is for work, study, social obligations or religious vocation – not for individual pleasure and adventure. Regardless, Ghanaians are hospitable and helpful to travellers, particularly outside Accra. As much of travel in Ghana happens on buses and trotros, one can quickly make many friends. Travellers receive many questions and offers of friendship, particularly in places where Ghanaians meet very few foreigners. In this way, travellers can be ground-level ambassadors of their culture. Ghanaians have long memories and will recall people they met from your country decades ago.

How Ghanaians Hear Foreigners

While Ghanaians are welcoming of foreign expertise and will naturally accord respect to foreigners, you should also be careful that you refrain from giving your opinion on everything and gaining a reputation of being *too known*[52]. To you, there are obvious solutions to issues of transportation, infrastructure, sanitation and business organization that come from elsewhere, but there are ways to communicate them tangentially and constructively[53]. While Ghanaians are critical of the challenges in their home country, Ghanaians are also proud and they will quickly tire of hearing about how things are done better elsewhere.

As a newcomer, you may have some difficulty understanding Ghanaian accents. This cuts both ways: speaking quickly or using slang can confuse a Ghanaian listener, so adjust your speaking accordingly. A Ghanaian may be too embarrassed to ask you to repeat what you have said or to clarify. If providing instructions, ask the person to repeat back what you have said to ensure that there is no misunderstanding.

How Ghanaians See Foreigners

Ghanaians take great pride in their appearance and judge others accordingly. Even those with little means taking a trotro to work will still take the time to dress in their finest, polishing their shoes and applying makeup. In spite of the equatorial sun and heat, Ghanaians can be seen in full suits or designer jeans. When it comes to work, the standard for women is smart, well-fitting clothes. Women typically dress conservatively, with covered shoulders and hemlines below the knees. For men, formal business attire is standard, including a tie, ironed shirt and shined shoes if possible.

Offices may observe Casual Friday, allowing for jeans and a simple top, such as a polo shirt. However, for both men and women, there is

---

[52] Too known = a know-it-all

[53] This will be discussed further in Managing and Leading Ghanaians.

also a tradition of Ghana Wear Friday, designed to promote Ghanaian printed fabrics and styles. This both allows people to demonstrate their national pride/solidarity, while also wearing something other than a suit or dress to the office or to public events. It can also be worn when meeting high-level government contacts, as even minsters appreciate the gesture.

For women, a loose-fitting top or dress in local fabric can be worn. For men, the standard "Friday shirt" is a boxy button-up collared shirt with short sleeves made from wax print or batik cotton, or a pull-over smock made of thick cotton particular to Northern Ghana. Everyone should have a go-to Friday shirt, if not a few.

These clothes can be purchased off the rack at a local store like Woodin, or made by a tailor/seamstress with fabrics chosen from the market. Tailored clothes are quite affordable, including linen shirts and slacks, which work well in the heat.

Foreigners should think twice about their casual clothes in Ghana. Shorts are to be worn by schoolboys. Ripped jeans and vintage t-shirts are for the club – or the farm. For women and men, shirts that expose the shoulders are not for the office. If unsure, best to dress on the more formal side.

The same goes for personal hygiene. Ghanaian women spend significant time and money on hairstyles, which change regularly. Ghanaian men, if they keep their hair and beard, keep them well-trimmed. Longer beards and dreadlocks are associated with Rastafari, which is not viewed highly by most Ghanaians. Your style may be unique and is your own, but know that you may be judged by it, particularly by professionals.

Bringing It All Together

Regardless of your best efforts, you will stand out in Ghana and occasional faux pas will happen. The good news is that Ghanaians will give you the benefit of the doubt. For your part, try to see yourself from a Ghanaian perspective and adjust your behaviour accordingly. If you are really unsure, engage your cultural translator for a second opinion. As always, approach new things with a sense of humility and openness to learn and you will find that Ghanaians will be open to you.

When you go somewhere, do not act superior to the people who live there.
-Akan proverb

Working with Ghanaians

Vignette #2: Shopping Mall, Accra

Taxis in Ghana still follow traditional commerce: unwritten rules, effective negotiation and a little bit of poker and theatre thrown in. To know how to haggle is a feeling of empowerment.

Recently returned to Accra, I stood in the sun with my family and our bags of groceries, trying to negotiate a reasonable taxi fare to return from the supermarket. The exasperated driver, displeased with his prospects, told me to go "over there" for my ride.

We walked up to a small parked taxi and a woman came and said, "Let's go!" She drove carefully, asked what radio station we preferred and even if we would like a little AC. Afterward, she helped with our child when we alighted.

We had stumbled on Esenam, possibly the only female taxi driver in Accra. She had just started and was trying to build her client base, cleverly taking the taxi union's castoffs and building a client base. In taking the low fare up front, she was playing the long game.

Naturally, we hired her again and recommended her to colleagues, who engaged her and shared her contact with other offices. Soon enough, she went from driving part-time, to driving full-time and chartering weekend trips, to training other female drivers, to consulting for international organizations looking to hire women in transportation projects. Last I saw her, she was featured on BBC and was a guest speaker at a conference headlined by heads of state. Talk about an effective negotiator!

Working with Ghanaians

Money Matters

To do business with Ghanaians, you should have an idea of how Ghanaians see money. How you value money is a reflection of your upbringing, your current status, your culture and other factors[54].

Consider the typical western cellphone user: Your provider offers two main payment options: For option one, you can sign up for a contract that provides you with a cellphone and a fixed monthly rate for talk, text and data. You could bundle with your internet, TV, home phone or other family members' plans to reduce your cost to the provider. Users with simple needs would go with option two, in which you buy a phone outright, pay-as-you-go and top up your phone periodically. If on contract, your costs are significant, but predictable and your company will send you a new smartphone when it is time to renew your contract.

Now consider the typical Ghanaian cell phone user: Your income is not steady, or is not received regularly, so you probably do not want a fixed monthly rate under a long-term contract. In fact, you would like to minimize costs as much as possible. And you would rather buy an off-brand or used phone on the street, or hope for a relative living abroad to bring a new smartphone on his next visit home. The phone can run on a SIM card and top-up credit that are both so cheap, people sell them in the market and on the street for a few cedi. You can make your credit last, since all calls on your company's network are free (and if the network signal is unreliable, simply get

---

[54] *Your Money or Your Life* by Vicki Robin and Joe Domniguez (2008) describes these different perspectives and how they influence people. The American authors conclude, "Money is something we choose to trade our life energy for." (P. 51) Many foreigners working in Ghana could benefit greatly from this book.

two numbers). What if you are low on credit, or want to delay buying more? If you think your friend has more, simply call their number, hang up and wait for them to call you back, using their credit (a practice known as *flashing*). If someone calls looking for a favour, you can avoid them by blaming lack of credit or signal. So now you have a phone and can use it for next to nothing.

The Ghanaian approach would at first seem inconceivable to a foreigner, but there are good reasons for this on a practical level with the cost of daily life in Ghana. There are also hints at Ghanaian cultural characteristics and values that inform the view and usage of money. Ghanaians will go to great lengths to delay costs, keep costs low or avoid costs altogether, while family and communal networks and tangential behaviours are used to one's advantage.

How Ghanaians See Money – The Art of the Hustle

If you are a typical westerner, money is seen as payment for effort, which is used to spend on essentials and things that make you happy. The general pattern is that money is scarce in your 20s and 30s, but as your career is established, you start to set personal and family financial goals pay back educational debts, eventually saving enough for a family, a house as well your hobbies and vacations. At a certain point, you expect to retire debt-free with your children grown up, perhaps sell your property and downsize so that you can enjoy your autumn years peacefully.

In Ghana, the view of money is quite different over one's lifetime. Growing up in a large family, limited resources must be shared, which means quality schooling, including post-secondary education is a luxury. Extended family members may be expected to help you out. This extends to after school, when you look for work through your network. You may also seek schooling abroad to earn a prestigious degree, foreign passport and maximize your earning potential back home. If you can earn a salaried job in the city and perhaps start a side-business, you can make enough to start a family, build a house and buy a car for the long commute.

Now that you are earning, you are expected to share with those who are in need: parents, siblings, aunts, uncles and cousins, school and medical fees, funerals, donations to church or mosque[55]. You may yourself still need to ask family for loans for major investments, since banks are not reliable. You avoid paying taxes and government "user fees" wherever possible. Life is a hustle: you always make sure that your shoes are shiny and your white shirts crisp.

If all goes well, you will become a respected member of your family, church and perhaps political party. As you age, your investment is the land and you rely on your prosperous children, perhaps your church and meager government benefits to supplement whatever savings you may have. Your success as a patriarch or matriarch earns you respect and honour and your funeral will be a massive affair, demonstrating your value.

These two scenarios could be summed up as the American Dream and the Ghanaian Dream. In both instances, you go through school, get a job, have kids and a family and retire, but the factors throughout are completely different. Thus, as the Ghanaian worldview is vastly different from the western worldview, it informs the Ghanaian perspective on money matters.

---

[55] Christians in many churches in Ghana are expected to tithe 10% of their income. Muslims also contribute zakat.

Ghanaian Networks

There are no islands in Ghana[56], and this extends to people. As Ghana develops, the middle class grows. However, wealth, power and privilege is relative: if you are just making ends meet but you are the best-off in your family (or a struggling student living abroad), as the wealthiest and most prosperous, you will have relatives phoning you at all hours looking for assistance.

In the communal Ghanaian culture, family is just about everything. To have a large family is to have a place to belong and a safety net, as the above example shows. If your father dies, your uncle can give you a job. If your mother dies, your auntie will take you in. This cuts both ways: you must also show generosity to your family and fulfill your duty if called upon. Family business matters are also common. On the other hand, Ghanaian trust of outsiders is low, which may be a reason why business mergers are rare. At the end of the day, if you need money, the government is not to be trusted, banks probably would not lend to you and even microfinance institutions are too demanding. The place you can always go to is your family.

This network extends beyond the family to community, ethnicity, religion and politics. There is a reason why chiefs regularly hold audiences and why government ministers have five cellphones that are always ringing: because someone is always in need of a favour.

The network also extends beyond Ghana: family and friends living abroad are expected to contribute financially, since they are believed to be earning plenty of dollars, pounds or euros. The reality is that Ghanaian students and workers abroad often struggle themselves to stay afloat. However, if they can fulfill their expectations, they will return a respected Big Man/Woman.

---

[56] To clarify: there *are* small islands in Ghana (in Lake Volta, the Volta River, Songor Lagoon, Keta Lagoon and near Busua), but they are quite miniscule and sparsely populated.

The persistence of poverty and large family networks means that the needs placed on the relatively well-off are heavy, as they are often at the top of a large pyramid. Many middle-class Ghanaians need to walk a fine line between individual prosperity and communal well-being.

In many cultures, family matters are often private matters, finances are rarely discussed openly and financial assistance is requested only by close family members or friends in dire situations. Indeed, talking about money is one of the biggest stressors for foreigners working with Ghanaians, as requests can seem quite commonplace. However, one must get used to this reality and be able to handle it effectively. One can stay blissfully ignorant by keeping the subject taboo, but knowing the situation of your Ghanaian colleagues and employees can help you to understand what motivates them.

Some Things Have Value, Others Do Not

Ghanaians see value where others may not. For example, the religious character of Ghanaians means that church and mosque are important parts of the social fabric of Ghana. In a country where government services are limited, the house of worship not only provides salvation, but security and prosperity in this life through safety nets.

Inversely, Ghanaians will not invest in something if they do not see any value in it. An example is opening a bank account. While a westerner sees a safe place to store money, invest and access capital (e.g. mortgage or line of credit), the average Ghanaian sees a company that charges monthly fees to do the same thing that a mattress can do. With annual interest rates starting around 25%, few Ghanaians are eligible for commercial loans and it is much easier to ask for money from a wealthy relative abroad who can send US dollars and who is much more flexible on payment terms.

Strategic Delaying

An important tool for Ghanaians is the art of strategic delaying. Foreigners will notice that when something is needed from a Ghanaian, there is often a reason why they are unavailable: they or a relative have been sick, they are travelling or their car broke down. Often, this is a legitimate reason, but it often is a tangential way of avoiding something unpleasant. This strategic delaying is at its best when it comes to money matters. The everyday accounting of life means people need to be creative with what little they have and stretch it for as long as possible. The Ghanaian economy seems to be funded by arrears, with everyone putting off a payment or building a tab while chasing down another.

Even the government is adept at strategic delaying. Any business will tell you that contracting with the District Assembly means waiting for payment for months, with regular calls to the District Chief Executive, his staff and other movers and shakers. In fact, assemblies often get their annual budget in November, which means a month of frenzied paying off of arrears before the cycle starts again in January.

Credit Traps

As someone at the top of the hierarchy, helping the less-fortunate is expected. If lending money to a Ghanaian, the process of getting it paid back can be arduous. It is not always possible to avoid this trap, but having reasonable expectations and effective safeguards can be helpful.

Working with Ghanaians

How can one avoid this trap? It is not always possible, but having reasonable expectations and effective safeguards can be helpful. First, it may not be repaid on schedule. For employees, a loan with a clear repayment schedule is required, sourced from wages. Second, some form of holdback is helpful to see it to term. Having collateral is best[57]. Finally, consider the possibility that it will end up becoming a gift and budget accordingly.

Organizations also employ strategic delaying to keep costs low and balance the books. If you can delay an expense until the next month, it can make this month's balance sheet look all the better.

Consequently, another credit trap for foreigners is at the business level. In Ghana, giving credit to customers is a common way to build a client base and it can be the only way for a business model to function, but it can cause some of the biggest headaches for businesses. If you are using your working capital to fund credit and chasing down debtors, it puts a strain on your financial and human resources and inhibits growth. Businesses and social enterprises providing services that involve credit need to design and test their models carefully, particularly when dealing with rural or low-income clients. There are untapped markets in Ghana from solar lamps and microcredit to real estate and value chain enterprise financing, but there are rarely easy solutions.

---

[57] One foreigner who had been previously burned by a debtor gave a generous loan to her new househelp who needed to assist her niece. Househelp sometimes leave the employer without warning, so the colleague visited the person and her niece at a birthday party to get to know the family. The message? "Nice to meet you. I know who you are and where you live. Don't think about deviating from our agreement." The loan was paid back in full.

Watching Your Money

Countless organizations, particularly businesses, have landed in Ghana and fail because they burn up their runway quickly before they can find a profitable model. And plenty of foreigners find themselves blowing their personal budget because of the unexpected costs of living and helping others. In any case, the golden rule is to watch your money.

A key element of this is negotiation. Without it, life in Ghana quickly becomes unbearably expensive and business unsustainable. However, understanding negotiation in the Ghanaian cultural context will help to understand how to thrive financially in Ghana.

"One cannot both feast and become rich."
-Akan proverb

"No food for lazy man."
-Common trotro bumper sticker

Negotiation

How important is negotiation in Ghana? It is part of the social and economic fabric, with communal, harmonious, tangential, prideful and hierarchical aspects – next to football, it could be the national sport! For you, the ability to effectively negotiate can make-or-break an expat's budget and start a successful business. Consider the following:

An expat decides to start a business in Ghana. Her European company gives her an annual salary of $100,000 (including travel allowance) and will reimburse her for all costs with receipts. She first finds an office to rent. Because there are few sources of info, she arrives in a hotel room and within the first two weeks, an agent helps her find a home/office combination in Labone near downtown with a monthly rent of $4,000 USD and a part-time gardener for $100/month. She also buys a generator from the dealership for $5,000, because electricity is unreliable. She buys $5,000 of furniture and appliances as well as two $2,000 laptops from the mall (whose stores give receipts) and gets unlimited internet for $100/month. She purchases a company car (a light SUV) new from the Toyota dealership for $32,000 and hires a driver for $1,000/month. She hires househelp to cook and clean part-time for $200/month, buys her groceries from the South African supermarket chain and eats at restaurants.

A Ghanaian decides to start a business in Ghana. She starts with a loan from her uncle and delays repayments for as long as possible. She starts her business from a church friend's house in Tema and promises to chip in for rent when it takes off. For internet, she buys credit and uses her cellphone as a hotspot for her slow and buggy laptop, which she got second-hand at the market. When electricity and internet both fail, she conducts business from the local internet cafe. For transportation, she takes trotros and the occasional taxi or hired truck until she's scraped enough money to buy a second-hand Tata pickup, which she drives herself. She eats chop and her mom's cooking throughout.

Which business is more likely to burn through its runway in the first six months? Which one is more likely to turn a profit?

The Ghanaian approach at first appears counter-intuitive. It requires so much more effort on the part of the businessperson and does not guarantee quality inputs. However, the key factor is that the expat has made all of her purchases at official prices using official services, as per the standard policy of her business. The Ghanaian has used her personal connections and her negotiating skills to keep her costs minimal. It is less efficient, but her burn rate will be much more modest and the business more likely to be competitive and sustainable in the long run.

The average expat businessperson would look at this and think, "Well this is ridiculous. You can't run a successful western business in Ghana." To a certain extent, this is true: the standard business model only works in a rare number of instances (e.g. Golden Tulip, DHL, KFC). However the best expat businesses are the ones that achieve their goals while keeping their costs low. There is a reason that Lebanese, Indian, Chinese, (and more recently South African and Brazilian) firms have a commanding local market share: they know how to set up, work hard and keep their overhead rates to a minimal level. Often this means working outside of the formal system. A foreigner may not always be able to do this in their business, but it is at least important to know how it works.

Negotiation: an Essential Skill

To state it plainly: negotiation is an essential skill for thriving in Ghana, as much as speaking English is an essential skill for thriving in Ghana. Whether formally in the boardroom or haggling on the street, negotiation is at the root of Ghanaian society and it will not be going anywhere soon. So learn how to haggle.

The Art of the Haggle

The economy is slowly formalizing and prices of some goods are set and visible to all (e.g. petrol, groceries and hotels), but most are not. Until the economy formalizes, haggling will be a critical method to do business from selling onions to large-scale contracts.

Consider haggling in the market: for most goods, the seller gives the initial offer at double the market rate while the buyer starts at half the market rate. The unspoken understanding is that an agreed-upon rate at or near the market rate will be achieved. For example, if haggling over a bag of tomatoes, the market rate will likely be 4 cedis. So the seller starts with an offer of 8 cedis, while the buyer starts with a counter of 2 cedis, eventually meeting up in the middle.

The most important thing to know when haggling: **know your desired price**. When you know this, you are a much more confident negotiator and more likely to achieve your goal. You can then plan your initial offer and guide the negotiations from there. Other important factors to success:

• Know if what you are looking to buy is an essential item or not. The best negotiation tool is knowing that you do not need the item for which you are negotiating[58].

---

[58] This is described well in Hélène Massicotte's Free to Pursue blog. http://www.freetopursue.com/blog/2016/8/18/what-kills-our-negotiation-power

- Like a gambler, know your limit beforehand. What is the maximum that you willing to pay?

- Know where else you can purchase the thing you want. You might want to get a few initial "quotes" to triangulate the market price of the item. If not possible, the seller has more leverage and you are bound to their pricing.

- Negotiations can be intense: Ghanaians almost yell at each other in argument, but once a price is reached, everyone is friends. So do not take it personally, be diplomatic and do not be vindictive. You can tell the seller that you don't want the "obruni price", but do not seriously play the race card and make a spectacle.

- When you want to give your final offer or know the seller's, say, "What is your best price?" This will force the seller to make a final offer.

- Negotiating is coming to an agreement that satisfies both parties. So if the price does not satisfy you, walk away. At this point, the seller may relent and take your final offer (this also works as an "extreme" negotiating tactic, but is risky). Otherwise, you can almost always find what you are looking for elsewhere.

- Key phrases in Twi: "me patcho, tisso" = "please, a little less" (on the price) and "entu swoh" = "give me a little extra" or "dash me" (especially for produce)

Haggling is exhausting for most expats, especially when one knows the price. When in a hurry to catch a taxi, if you give the final offer straight away, the driver may take it, but feel disappointed that the social element has been stripped away (and the sport is gone from the activity!).

Positions of Strength and Weakness

There is a delicate power balance between the local vendor and the foreign buyer:

1) The local vendor is often working on slim margins and earns a meager income, so a foreign buyer could be an important source of income, especially if they are willing to pay a higher price (or do not know the market rate).

2) The foreign buyer is comparatively wealthy and is more likely to buy more than the average Ghanaian, but does not want to be seen as a source of easy cash or a sucker.

So, as a foreigner, remember that while you want to pay a fair price for your goods, most vendors are of modest means, so do not use your position in the hierarchy to inflict a price that causes the vendor to lose money. At the end of the day, the local vendor is more dependent on the transaction than the expat buyer and is probably looking to establish a long-term relationship with their new customer. If you inflict damage on your opponent regularly, you could get a reputation in the market for being cruel and unfair and sour relations in the business community. Sometimes, even when you win, you can still lose.

Whatever the case, know when you are in a position of strength or weakness. Often as an expat, you will naturally be calling the shots and the seller will be highly motivated to get your business. On the other hand, if there is only one guy in town selling solar inverters and your operation will grind to a halt without one immediately, you will be at his mercy. If you have little or no leverage, using your interpersonal skills will be essential to avoid getting fleeced!

Negotiation at the Organizational Level

Office relations are a delicate balance of diplomacy and while there is not outright haggling, there is plenty of deal-making under the surface. When hiring staff, remuneration may or may not be up for negotiation, particularly at an embassy where positions and salary are fixed. As a bargaining chip, you could emphasize the benefits of the work or find out if you can offer extra responsibilities or files that speak to the candidate's interests, desires and personal pride[59].

When negotiating with other organizations, the same principles apply, but the process may take longer and the stakes may be higher. There may also be more room for creativity. For example, you may be able to make concessions that have significant value to the other party using your internal resources, like providing a sponsorship opportunity for an event and hosting it on your organization's premises.

An exception to this is Requests for Proposals (RFPs) and Requests for Quotations (RFQs). In these cases, the prospects for negotiation are quite slim in an open competition with fixed criteria. This can make the process quite cutthroat. Some competing firms may be prepared to leverage personal connections or offer illicit incentives to the requestor to gain an upper-hand. This is prevalent in RFPs, where there is often significant room for interpretation and where intangible factors can play a decisive role in a winning bid. On the other hand, RFQs can be more straightforward. If the item or service demanded is uniform or straightforward, there is less room for interpretation and the best price is more likely to win.

---

[59] This will be discussed further in Managing and Leading Ghanaians.

So How Do You Negotiate in Ghana?

Let us say you are seeking to locally purchase a company vehicle. The first step is *know what you want, know your price and know where to get it.* You decide that a new light SUV might be best, but that a late-model version would suffice. You set a budget and your upper limit for what is your preferred price. You also look into dealerships and private sellers. You find a recently-imported vehicle that suits your needs listed at a price in your budget from a Lebanese firm. Your second step is *diplomatic negotiations.* You arrange a visit to view the vehicle and perhaps bring your mechanic along to assist with the inspection. Pleasantries are exchanged before getting into the discussion. A part will need to be replaced and this will need to be done by you, so you make a low-ball offer. The seller tells you that it is well below what is possible, but comes down a bit from the listed price. After careful consideration, you decide that you really would like the vehicle but only at a certain rate, so you *give your final price,* ready to walk away. If the seller accepts, you *agree on the deal,* transfer process and terms of payment. With this, you not only have a vehicle but you have *established a personal relationship* with the seller. Once your business expands, you will know that you can contact the seller for more vehicles and possibly get the inside track on another good deal.

Next Steps: Using Your Intercultural Skills in Ghana

With an understanding of how culture works, the particular hallmarks of Ghanaian culture, how Ghanaians see foreigners, how they see money and how to negotiate, you can start to think about how **you** can work interculturally with Ghanaians. The following chapters will give an idea on how to work with, lead and manage Ghanaians – whether in business, an embassy, non-governmental organization or other setting. These have been developed based on the experiences of foreigners and Ghanaians alike and while every situation is different, you may find that certain points resonate or can apply to your case.

Good soup draws people to itself.
-Ewe proverb

Establishing an Organization

Consider the previous chapter's example of an expat setting up a business in Ghana with a western mentality and budget. Not only is it too expensive to be profitable or competitive in the local market, but it also bears a great deal of additional risks. How can she be sure that she is making strategic and sustainable decisions? What about when it is time to hire staff? How can she be sure that she is picking the right people and building a corporate culture of integrity?

Establishing a formal business, non-governmental organization or social enterprise in Ghana is challenging and is not for the timid or faint of heart. To quote the brother of the founder of Koforidua-based off-grid energy company Burro, "while there is a business to be made… it's not a get-rich quick scheme. It's not for people who wither in the heat, worship Wi-Fi, and like their food cooked just so."[60] This chapter provides an overview of challenges for entrepreneurs and leaders looking to start an organization or establish an office in Ghana.

First off, though Ghana is an informal economy, one will still find no shortage of administrative hurdles and red tape. A recommended source of information is the trade section of your country's embassy or high commission. Their goal is to open up business opportunities for their citizens, which in turn grows their own economy, so they are often quite happy to help. Ghanaians can often work under the table and avoid business taxation for some time, but a highly-visible foreigner may not, so take advantage of this information. PriceWaterhouseCoopers also has tax compliance resources updated annually. A wealth of information and resources can be found in

---

[60] Alexander, Max. *Bright Lights, No City.* Hyperion, New York. 2012. P. 373

Your Essential Guide on Moving to Ghana by Ivy Prosper, who relocated to Ghana to successfully start her own business. Also, seek out people who know the industry and are willing to share. Remember that while you may have a unique idea or plan, someone else has probably tried something similar from which you can learn. As the world experiments with remote working, the environment continues to evolve.

Making a Plan and Sequencing

It sounds obvious, but you will need a plan. Figure out what your staffing and procurement needs will be, including preparing an organizational chart.

Unless you have deep experience working in Ghana or in the region, foreign entrepreneurs recommend that you start with the nucleus of your founders and make your initial hire a strong Ghanaian office administrator who can do the hard work of navigating local hiring and procurement[61] and keep the office running. This critical addition will allow you to build the team outward and scale up.

Shiny Things vs. Needed Things

In a proud and hierarchical culture, projecting an image of professionalism and success is highly desired (and for some, seen as essential to be taken seriously). For this reason, firms often start with their branding and promotional needs before the hard work of operating a functioning business. This may work in some high-performance industries, but in most cases, it is better to start small and grow organically. Do you need a flagship office or just a room

---

[61] Recall that there is often an "obruni price". A local administrator can also negotiate on local terms, which can lead to far better deals on procurement.

with reliable electricity and internet? Or perhaps only a virtual presence is needed? Do you need a new Land Cruiser, or will a used RAV4 do? Employees may also expect perks like new laptops and smartphones, so set their expectations to maintain harmony. Make sure that any "ask" is justified on the basis of value for money.

Finding Space

Finding office space is a challenge in itself. Leasing is most common. In Ghana, landlord/tenant relations are mostly unregulated and unmonitored. This has led to a system in which a renter is expected to pay between one and three years' rent in advance. Landlords are also not responsible for services like maintenance and renovations as in western countries. Renting housing and office space is a profitable business and landlords may live abroad and have property managers working on their behalf. You may choose to engage a real estate agent who knows how to navigate the system, but be clear on your needs: buildings range from shabby colonial-era buildings to ostentatious villas and modern high-rise office space. Agents will want to sell you what they think you need, which usually leans towards the ostentatious villas, when something more modest and affordable will do. Non-commercial space tends to be much more affordable than commercial space.

So choose your space wisely, make sure you know what maintenance or renovations will be required and who is responsible for it. Negotiate well and ensure that you have the funds to provide the deposit and keep your organization afloat. In Accra, rents can be astronomical.

Buying land is another challenge altogether. As noted, land ownership is a complex matter. First, ensure that the land is genuinely the seller's to give. The ubiquitous "THIS HOUSE IS

NOT FOR SALE" graffiti exists for good reason. Obtain proof of ownership from the Ministry of Local Government and Rural Development. Second, understand if the land can be sold or only leased. In many areas, land is communal and held in trust by the chief. In this case, it can be leased for up to ninety-nine years. Also, once land is purchased, assert your claim by building immediately. If someone else tries to build on your land or has a competing claim based on traditional practices, getting them off the land will take a long time.

With all of this in mind, working remotely is an option that may seem attractive, but consider all factors, as physical space may still be essential to effectively conduct daily business. For a small office or startup looking to have a light touch but also maintain a physical presence and access to resources, tech hubs and co-working spaces are increasingly popular and can be found in all major Ghanaian cities, including Accra, Tema, Kumasi, Takoradi and even Tamale.

Finding People

Finding the right people takes time and effort. Building a team can be done quickly, but the long-term consequences can be significant and harmful to your organization. However, take the time to effectively screen your candidates and find the right talent and you will have a much greater chance of success.

Knowing in advance what kind of people you want is critical. Are you looking to bring in like-minded experts from abroad? Or are you looking to fully tap into Ghanaian talent[62]? In between, there is a sizeable population of non-indigenous Ghanaians of Lebanese,

---

[62] This is not a trivial question. Bringing in a foreigner to do a job that a Ghanaian can do is more expensive, often less efficient and in the long-run, less effective and sustainable as a solution. The default option should be going local, unless an exception is required.

Indian, Chinese and Korean origin as well as mixed-race Ghanaians who have their own intercultural understandings and strengths[63].

Hiring

The labour market in Ghana is very large for both skilled and unskilled persons. The university system alone churns out thousands of new graduates each year and many more are returning from studies abroad. However, that does not mean that hiring employees is an easy task, nor should it be farmed out. Lax hiring practices can lead to homogeneous organizations without ethnic and gender diversity. It is possible to hire quickly based on CVs and short interviews, but selecting the wrong person has major long-term repercussions. CVs can be misleading, falsified or prepared by a third party. Candidates may say all the right answers or talk a good game, so ask questions to know their motivations and their opinions on values and ethics[64]. Just as important are reference checks to get a second (and third) opinion on a candidate. Providing a reference to a poor candidate can harm one's own reputation, so they are not given lightly. Another recommended strategy is to give a test to a candidate. For example, one could request a mock presentation on the company's line of business to see how a candidate prepares, analyses, writes, provides recommendations and presents. Foreign and Ghanaian professionals alike confirm: taking the time to

---

[63] Non-indigenous communities in Ghana have been traditionally formed a successful business class, including import-export, real estate, restaurants, hotels and shopping centres. Working with people from these communities could be an effective early move, particularly for people who can deal effectively with contractors and bureaucracy (see the reference to the "golden key" further in this chapter).

[64] A simple but critical question is: *why do they want the job?* For many Ghanaians getting the office job is the goal itself, rather than the starting point to building their career and achieving success for the organization.

properly screen a candidate is time-consuming, but is also the most effective strategy.

An effective hiring board includes Ghanaians and foreigners to screen candidates from multiple cultural perspectives and to avoid opportunities for foreign or Ghanaian nepotism. Special care should be taken to consider candidates to ensure a gender balance, as women can often be screened out on technicalities, regardless of their potential. As noted earlier, foreigners broadly agree that hiring Ghanaian women is a smart choice, producing hard-working, loyal and motivated employees without links to established patronage networks. Hiring by ethnicity or religion is not encouraged, but do seek to have diversity in the office. Finally, young candidates may be less experienced, but often have a drive to succeed rather than to simply get the job with the title (which is common). Younger employees are also more likely to buy into and promote a dynamic workplace culture and embrace change. With these in mind, you will be able to more effectively screen ideal candidates.

An important intangible factor is a candidate's ability to know the terrain, use their network and build contacts and relationships. This is particularly important in organizations that are working with the bureaucracy. This "golden key" will open many important doors. On the other hand, candidates with intimate knowledge of the sector or a long history of working within the bureaucracy may be difficult and inflexible employees, so proceed carefully.

Negotiating a salary depends on your organization's budget, salary structure, equity opportunities and other factors. Embassies, for example, will have fixed salary bands, so a candidate may be disappointed to know that it is not negotiable. However, ensure that candidates also know the additional benefits of the job, whether it be opportunities for travel, overtime remote working or further skills development. Also, in Ghana, a 13th month bonus is common, so inquire about the practice before meeting with candidates.

Few candidates come fully prepared and trained for the work. Learning is a continuous process, so be sure to identify where you perceive any gaps that can be remedied in the short term. You can also discuss with a new employee their career goals and where they would like to gain experience through training, learning and even travel opportunities.

Even an ideal candidate may be a bad fit in practice. Having a trial employment period will help to ensure that you both are comfortable with the arrangement and that the organization is not stuck with the wrong employee long-term.

Now that Everything Is in Place

Once you have hired your employees and set up your space, you will need to set your rules and expectations for them as you build your corporate culture. This will take time and a wide variety of your intercultural skills. The next chapter will discuss this further.

A single tree cannot make a forest.
-Ewe proverb

Working with Ghanaians

Managing and Leading Ghanaians

An expat manager was brought to Ghana on a two-year assignment to manage a branch office that had operated for over two decades and was known as a pleasant office, but with major productivity issues and was known for not meeting the organization's global standards. Within a month, the manager issued directives to get the office up to the standards and things immediately changed. Office costs were slashed and two employees were terminated for serious misconduct. Yet over the ensuing months, productivity slowly dropped, absenteeism increased and some long-time employees with essential corporate memory departed to other organizations. At the end of the assignment, the manager was promoted, but his successor inherited a dysfunctional, demotivated staff with a broken office culture and was immediately distrusted by all Ghanaians.

How could someone doing the "right" thing according to widely-accepted international standards create such havoc? The following chapter will illustrate strategies to find effective, long-term solutions to intercultural working challenges[65].

Setting Expectations

It is often that a foreigner working with an organization will find him/herself managing personnel. This applies across the spectrum, from the corporate director managing a regional office in Accra down to the NGO volunteer advising a local farmer co-op in Bolgatanga. Even those who do not have people in their formal

---

[65] This chapter takes a great deal of inspiration from Stephen Covey's *The 7 Habits of Highly Effective People*.

employ will find themselves in a position of influence. For better or for worse, foreigners (particularly light-skinned ones) are commonly viewed as people who have power, whether in money, knowledge or connections.

Effective management of personnel is an important skill[66] and applying it in the Ghanaian cultural context is an additional challenge. Even more challenging is demonstrating effective leadership[67].

This chapter discusses managing Ghanaians throughout the employee life-cycle beyond hiring, including managing and firing. How it will apply to you depends on the context, as every workplace is different and every profession has its peculiarities. So this chapter is no substitute for consulting trusted sources with experience in your sector in Ghana as well as cultural translators, but consider these opinions informed by the experiences of foreign and Ghanaian managers.

Managing Styles in Ghana

Broadly speaking, there are two extremes of managing Ghanaians. The first is directive: you are the boss and what you say, goes. The second is consensual: we are all equals and in it together.

---

[66] Indeed, many foreign professionals are thrust into management situations for the first time in Ghana. Management skills are both learned and acquired, so consider reflecting on your own management style.

[67] Note that leadership and management are often conflated, but are two very different things. Leadership is about defining a vision and ensuring that the organization is oriented towards it. Management is ensuring that the organization's people and resources are used to achieve this vision. In the words of Peter F. Drucker, "Management is doing things right; leadership is doing the right things." (Covey, P. 101)

Managers who are directive may need to be in industries like construction and manufacturing where specifications need to be exact and deadlines need to be met. However, directive managers are often so because they do not trust anyone. They quickly become frustrated and accuse staff of laziness and incompetence. Managers then become directive to ensure that goals can be met and that their staff (who cannot be trusted) need to be constantly monitored and restrictions set on them. This will help in the immediate term with outputs and meeting deadlines, but it eventually leads to a vicious cycle of mistrust and cynicism in their employees. Consequently, the staff learn to fear and mistrust the boss and to lose any respect. Work becomes simply a matter of being present and doing the bare minimum, if only when the boss is around. The organization's equipment becomes fair game for misuse and theft, justified as compensation for their manager's harshness. Employee turnover increases when people find something better (or less bad). What are the chances of an organization's long-term success under these conditions?

On the other extreme, managers who are consensual lead offices and dynamic distributed teams. They value input and do not make decisions without consulting employees and give them leeway to pursue their interests, assuming that it will benefit the organization over the long term. They also make friends with their employees. Over time, deadlines are missed, goals are not achieved and employee productivity slows as side-projects take over. The productive ones and ones not dedicated to the organization's mission leave for greener pastures. How can an organization survive and compete under these conditions?

This thinking applies to managers worldwide, but has a particular flavour in Ghana. Directive managers complain about their Ghanaian employees in all of the ways above and reinforce colonial thinking that "we" need to manage "them" and show them the "proper way" that things are done, bringing in foreigners to police them. This reinforces racial and cultural prejudices. On the other hand, consensual managers are lulled into a sense of complacency with their seemingly-warm and friendly Ghanaian employees. Wanting to integrate, they work harder at being friends, overlooking issues and forgetting to be managers, let alone leaders. Both types misread Ghanaian culture and fail to use its strengths by operating within a culturally-relevant framework.

The directive style is the standard in Ghana. For Ghanaians who think hierarchically and desire harmony, the boss is the boss and the employee is there to implement their will. However, in Ghana, it leads to personality-based organizations that unquestioningly follow a leader and do not build leadership skills, confidence or critical thinking in their people, so when the leader leaves, retires or dies, the organization quickly decays. In Ghana, there are countless small firms, hotels and restaurants that slowly fall apart after a change in leadership until they inevitably close down, becoming only distant memories. There are also many examples of local branches of international firms investing heavily in a local presence, trying to replicate their consensual-style home office with Ghanaian staff and financially bleeding themselves dry over time.

Somewhere between the directive and consensual approaches is an effective third way – one that recognizes the peculiarities of Ghanaian culture while also harnessing them to build effective organizations. This third way is harder, takes more work and is not foolproof, but it is the more sustainable and successful path, as firms are discovering in Ghana. In particular, as companies and NGOs seek to indigenize their leadership and rely less on foreigners, this approach makes sense in the long term. It also has roots in Ghanaian culture: in most traditional societies in Ghana, the chief is a first among equals and makes decisions in discussion with other elders.

Working with Ghanaians

The challenge for many foreigners is to both assert their authority while also giving agency to their Ghanaian employees towards personal and professional growth, strengthening the organization as a whole. The following points will help to strike this balance.

Building a Team

Whether assembling a team or inheriting one from your predecessor, building the team you want will take time, more so in an intercultural environment. So seek first to understand the environment and the people. Take the time to analyze the situation critically and learn more about your employees and colleagues. This starts with getting to know them, what drives and motivates them and what experience and strengths they bring to the team. Seasoned foreign professionals confirm that the cultural complexities are deep and nuanced in the Ghanaian workplace and that there is much hidden to the untrained eye that will take a long time to perceive and understand.

Once you have conducted your analysis, you can then seek to be understood by your Ghanaian employees and colleagues. Never assume that your colleagues know or understand you or your culture, even if they have worked for you and your compatriots for years. You will need to communicate your own culture as well as the work culture that you wish to build. A seminar, team retreat or cultural experience could be an opportunity to discuss these issues in depth communally while reaching a decision on the way forward endorsed by the leader. For example, if you are trying to instill a western standard of customer service, take the time to talk not only about the expectations of employees, but talk about why this standard exists and why you believe that it is the most effective style for your organization. Then discuss and agree on how employees and managers can implement this vision.

This should not be seen as a one-off experience or transfer of knowledge, but as a longer-term process that helps to establish and nurture relationships and deepen intercultural understanding.

Motivating Your Team

Successful teams worldwide do not motivate employees through fear and coercion, but through getting them to subscribe to the organization's vision and motivating them appropriately. If you can allow them to contribute to the vision, they have the opportunity to personally invest in it and have a sense of ownership in the organization. Foreign and Ghanaian professionals agree that this is equally relevant in Ghana as elsewhere.

The desire for harmony by Ghanaians applies to the office culture. Reinforce social bonds by greeting each of your employees in the morning and perhaps asking about their health and their family. If an employee sends an important e-mail, send a thank you as a courtesy. Rituals are important, so do not discount them. Figure out what they are and how they fit into the existing organizational culture, whether it is celebration of birthdays, weekly tea breaks or team lunch[68]. If the team appears to have too many regular meetings, ask questions to find out why. If they have ideas for building the team spirit, listen to them and consider them thoughtfully.

How an organization's workspace functions is an indicator of its culture. In the case of embassies and high commissions, walking into one is like walking out of Ghana and into the country itself, not only in the physical appearance, but the change in behaviours and norms. You may not be able to (nor should you) replicate your home office

---

[68] In Ghanaian culture, people high up in the hierarchy are expected to take care of their people, so managers should expect to pay for certain group activities or team lunches. In a similar way, one who invites another for drinks or a meal is expected to pay, unless otherwise understood.

in Ghana, but see what you can bring that will make it more effective. Figure out how to set up the workspace for your organization in a way that motivates your employees.

Autonomy and Proactivity

A key element to an effective organization is building an autonomous and proactive mindset in employees. The hierarchical nature of most Ghanaian organizations leads to a fear of decision-making and independent, critical thinking. In such offices, decisions are to be made by the boss and when the boss is out of the office, the decisions will wait until the boss' return. Nobody trusts the employees to make decisions themselves and they do not dare to start something without the boss' explicit approval. Inversely, foreign professionals may come from cultures that delegate authorities and responsibilities, favouring proactive "self-starters" that can get ahead on tasks and advance goals themselves, rather than waiting for instructions. In this culture, managers will support their employees, asking, "How can I support you to do what you want to do?" while also commanding, "Don't bring me a problem; bring me a solution."

This style requires significant trust and letting go by managers, particularly in an intercultural environment, but it also allows them to focus their limited time on high-value work rather than dealing with the problems of subordinates. The manager can set individual rolling work plans that feed into the team's strategic priorities. This takes time, including individual coaching and follow-up, but it builds more effective employees and teams in the long-run.

Time Management

On the other hand, a common challenge for managers is setting deadlines that can be respected and met. In the Ghanaian workplace, this is compounded by GMT. As noted earlier, there are intercultural solutions that can help build a work culture that adheres to time management principles and respects the sanctity of deadlines.

This rising tide may not lift all boats in your organization, so adjust your style on a person-by-person basis and plan for this over the longer term. Building proactivity and trust in employees will reduce the amount of work required by you as a manager and leader. However, this may take time.

When working -outside of your organization, GMT can only be mitigated through regular follow-up that in other cultures would be considered overbearing or even harassing. If you are dependent on a contractor or supplier meeting a deadline, check in regularly for an update on progress, remind them of why your work is important to them and ask detailed questions to ensure that there is no tangential response – better to find out about problems in advance than at the deadline.

Working Remotely

Office working culture is shifting rapidly: with better connectivity tools and faster internet, not all work needs to be done at the office. Will your employees want to work from home? What about you?

The desire to work remotely depends on the nature of the work and the personal circumstances and temperament of the worker. Does the employee have a long commute to the office? Must they juggle family schedules, like school/daycare or dinner preparation (tasks typically done by mothers)? Does their work require deep focus? If so, the option to work from home partially (or even fully) might seem like an appealing option. However, on a technical level, remote work typically requires stable electricity[69], a solid internet connection and the technology to enable work, like a laptop, smartphone and productivity tools. Without even one of these elements, working from home may be unfeasible. Socially, the office can be an important place for information sharing, networking, reinforcing personal bonds and collaborating. Recall the importance of those office rituals.

There is a trust element to remote work: managers must have faith that their employees are *actually* working. As a manager, one can apply the adage of "trust, but verify". Agree on the parameters, including the tasks, the objectives and the indicators that will measure them. For example, if an employee wants to work at home to prepare a document, agree that they will send the draft at the end of the day.

This can be an iterative process. If there is a standing agreement for remote working (e.g. one day per week), then set a time when the arrangement can be reviewed to ensure that it works for the manager, the employee and the rest of the team.

Getting and Giving Feedback

Building a team spirit that includes feedback is difficult but rewarding. Ghanaians prefer a harmonious approach and operate tangentially, avoiding uncomfortable situations and bearing any bad news. Yet how will you be able to garner reliable feedback from your people to avoid problems and to make improvements?

---

[69] The Electricity Company of Ghana is known by its initials *ECG*, which locals will say also stands for "Electricity Comes and Goes", or "Either Candle or Generator"!

When you are providing feedback to your colleagues and employees, provide it in a constructive manner that will be best understood. Take your time: storytelling in Ghana is an art and a skill. If you are looking to provide negative feedback to address a long-term or delicate issue, a Ghanaian approach would be to find the right time and start slowly, not rushing to confrontation or discussing all in one sitting. If the feedback is highly critical, you may also wish to engage a respected elder or third person on the team who can relay messages more effectively.

If you are unsatisfied with a response or concerned that it may not be providing a complete picture, ask the question again in a different manner, or ask for more details. You may be able to better identify the problem and follow it to the root. Your employee may also be telling you something in coded language and is expecting you to read between the lines.

If your culture is direct, explain why it is so and how your colleagues will be able to better understand it. With this information, they will be better able to empathize with you. They may be more confident in bringing their challenges to you or even admitting a mistake, rather than you finding out when it becomes a full-blown crisis.

Resolving Conflict

Ghanaians are highly social and try to maintain harmonious relations, but tensions in the office are inevitable. Things are rarely what they seem on the surface, so stay alert. If a conflict arises, try to determine whether the problem is as it seems on paper or if there is a deeper, hidden issue. The tangential nature of Ghanaian culture means that a foreigner may have difficulty getting a direct answer to a direct question, so try to seek the same information through different questions and assemble the needed response. Getting to the source of a conflict can take time and effort, with many questions needed to help peel back the layers.

If 90% of any relationship is communication, then most conflicts are a result of poor communication. When intercultural issues arise, the first thing to ascertain is if there was a miscommunication or misunderstanding. Discuss the matter with colleagues until it is resolved to your mutual satisfaction. If an intercultural issue appears intractable and compromise or consensus is not possible, it may require a firm decision. In all cases, maintain a respectful tone and do not show anger as you will lose the respect of your Ghanaian colleagues, no matter how right you may be.

Important to remember is that there are hidden systems and hierarchies in any office that are unknown to you but are well-understood by local colleagues. The decisions you make can throw these off balance. For example, a driver pool may ostensibly have a number of drivers and vehicles who are available to all personnel on demand, but informally, there may be an established order. Or in the case of a personnel change, a vacated office may be officially "open", but it is understood by Ghanaian colleagues that it "belongs" to a particular person.

The challenge is to know which battles to pick: some challenges are intractable and some systems so entrenched that the effort to change them may not be worth the effort required. And if your contract or assignment is limited and you are leaving soon, things may quickly change back to the way they were. The choice to engage or not is yours.

As with providing feedback, having difficult conversations is also an art and skill[70]. A tool that Ghanaians use to resolve conflict is the

---

[70] An excellent resource is another management literature classic: *Difficult Conversations: How to Discuss What Matters Most* by Douglas Stone, Bruce Patton and Sheila Heen.

trusted third party, which is a traditional dispute mechanism. Typically this is a village or family elder, while in the office, this could be a senior or relatively neutral party in the office who is approached to discuss the issue with the quarrelling parties separately as a form of shuttle diplomacy and find a resolution.

In extreme cases, issues can become deeply personal and even veer into the spiritual. As noted, unexplained or intractable problems may lead to supernatural explanations or solutions. If a conflict starts to take this dimension, be certain of the facts and record them to reduce the potential for hearsay and innuendo to take over the narrative. Remember that the situation may appear irrational and the solution rational to you, but it may not be the case for your colleagues. Do consult with trusted Ghanaian and non-Ghanaian colleagues on how to address the issue in a culturally appropriate way.

Building Integrity and Avoiding Corruption in Your Organization

Ghanaians see corruption on a daily basis: from the top, where government ministers with means well beyond the salary of a public servant interact with businesses flush with cash from sweetheart contracts down to the police officer looking for a dash to resolve a traffic infraction. Corruption takes many forms and is both a means for some to achieve riches and for others to avoid poverty. Yet no culture is inherently corrupt; it is only institutions that can become corrupted. The key is to build and maintain an organization's integrity[71].

Your organization's exposure to corruption depends on the nature of its work as well as how it operates. Anywhere one goes, there are

---

[71] This is a view espoused by Oxford professor Declan Hill in *The Fix: Soccer and Organized Crime*, which includes a case study on Ghanaian professional footballers.

three major factors than enable fraud: 1) opportunity for fraud, 2) motivation or pressure to commit fraud, and 3) a rationale or justification.

How can one avoid this?

1) Reduce the opportunities for fraud. Ensure that your organization has adequate checks and controls. On the financial side, ensuring that there are multiple financial control points (e.g. separate officers responsible for purchase authorization, commitment and verification) as well as records of goods (e.g. invoices for goods, asset inventories) and travel (e.g. vehicle logs, fuel records, GPS tracking). The goal is to build a compliance culture. However, beware of the perils of going overboard: the University of Ghana's Balme Library kept all books under lock and key, which drastically reduced theft, but also the number of readers.

2) Reduce the motivation and pressure to commit fraud. An employee who is invested in the organization is less likely to commit acts that harm it. Pressure is often an outside factor: particularly when one person many be an entire family's breadwinner. The least that an organization can do is provide a salary and benefits package that is commensurate with a middle-class Ghanaian lifestyle. Salary is often a major budget line for an organization, but it is better than funds leaking elsewhere.

3) Reduce the rationale and justification for fraud. Similar to motivation, an easy justification to commit fraud is that it is a victimless crime[72], particularly for large, well-funded organizations. If your people are paid and treated well by the organization, the rationale and justification weakens.

---

[72] White-collar crime is also seen as less serious by many Ghanaians than outright theft: if someone skims thousands of cedis from their organization and shares with their family, they are providing. Yet if someone on the street robs someone of their cellphone, there is a chance of violent mob justice or a lengthy prison term.

Most importantly, corruption is enabled by weak organizational culture and hindered by strong organizational culture. Build a culture of integrity in your organization. Keep them invested in the long-term vision of the organization. Remind your employees of the valuable work you do and its contribution to the socio-economic betterment of Ghana. On a practical level, build a rapport and trust between employees and management. Nobody likes to be a victim of theft, so if you build a sense of employee ownership in your organization, there will be a greater desire to protect its integrity.

Regardless, there are those who are keen to take advantage of the system, often in partnership. Foreign professionals confirm that unethical practices are often difficult to detect and culprits hard to pin down.

Firing

Not every employee is the right fit for the job and some will be completely wrong. In addition, the expansion and contraction of the economy or of project funding and other conditions can cause employees to be redundant. Terminating employment is something that should be exercised thoughtfully and carefully, no matter the conditions. In Ghanaian culture, it is taboo to bring bad news to a person and one must be respectful at all times, even during difficult conversations. One's job is a source of their personal pride and a demonstration of their worth – particularly for men.

First, when hiring an employee, a best practice is to start with a trial period lasting up to a few months to observe the employee in practice to ensure that the organization has not made a mistake. If the organization decides not to take on the employee permanently, provide adequate advance notification to the person. Provide feedback in a respectful manner and be sure not to focus on deficiencies, but note the strengths and recommend areas for improvement.

Terminating a worker's employment can be difficult personally and professionally for both the employee and manager as well. If letting go of employees due to downsizing or redundancy, do it over time and gently. A person who knows that it is coming and that it is not immediate will be more likely to accept the situation and to look for opportunities elsewhere. Saving face is important and the person being let go should be accorded respect throughout the process. Labour laws in Ghana are quite strong and Ghanaian employees are more likely to know them than their foreign managers. Combined with an employee's connections, it could make for a difficult process.

If terminating an employee immediately for misconduct, prepare carefully. First, ensure that there is a very strong justification[73] and no ambiguity of the rationale. Document the facts and build your case. Meet immediately with the employee and state your case and what will happen. You can either be directive, or present options for the employee: a clever employee may resign before being fired to save face and take severance pay. In any case, the terminated employee should be immediately removed from the organization's premises, returning identification, any keys or other items that could be a security hazard. Terminated Ghanaian employees are not likely to retaliate, but ensure that there is no room for them to do so, as a person with a deeply-wounded pride without a source of income can do extreme things[74].

---

[73] If your organization has a relevant policy and procedure, be sure to follow this.

[74] From a security perspective, terminated employees are a major source of crimes against foreigners. Dismissed security guards and househelp in particular have been convicted of engaging in or abetting theft, breaking-and-entering and even kidnapping of their former employers.

Terminations have social repercussions as well. Firing an employee is considered a major sign of disrespect and cuts to the core of one's pride. It also disrupts the social fabric of the organization. This may seem secondary to the major issue at hand (such as the employee's misconduct), but it leads to behaviours that surprise foreigners: colleagues are more likely to demonstrate solidarity with a colleague than to blow the whistle and may even implore that the manager reconsider the decision and administer a less severe punishment to save face and maintain organizational harmony. A third party may come to you to plead the case of the employee – this could be a colleague or even an elder of high social stature who knows little about the facts of the matter but is bound to speak on behalf of the offender and ask for leniency and a second chance, like a defense lawyer[75]. This is a ritual and if you are engaged, you need to participate. Do listen to the third party respectfully and attentively, even if you have privately made a firm decision. You will need to explain and justify your decision to employees to ensure that there is full understanding of the misconduct and the appropriateness of the punishment.

A Final Note: Choose Your Battles Wisely

Remember when coming into a new position that you are new, but your employees and colleagues have likely been in place for some time. They may have seen managers come and go and even when managers challenge the office status quo, they are likely to outlast you. So choose your battles wisely. To paraphrase Reinhold Niebuhr,

---

[75] This can be particularly tricky, as the elder is duty bound to help the person (whether the elder likes the person or not!) and is using his or her social standing as a collateral of sorts. If so, even if your decision is final, you may need to promise to reconsider the matter to satisfy the elder that they have presented their case and that you have listened to them. Otherwise, this shows disrespect to the elder and to the community as a whole.

learn to accept the things you cannot change, have the courage to change the things you can and have the wisdom to know the difference.

One head is not a council.
-Akan proverb

Working with Ghanaians

Doing Business with Ghanaians

An NGO received a contract to install a communal water pump in a rural community. The expat project manager talked to the government authorities who agreed that it was a good idea. The manager travelled to the community for a day visit, talked to the elders, led a community sensitization meeting and everyone agreed that it was a good idea and agreed on the site proposed by the NGO. After months of inquiries and a courtesy call to the regional minister, the government authorities approved the project and recommended a local borehole driller with experience in the area who could do the job. Eventually, it was constructed and the contract was completed.

The director of the NGO joined the public launch of the well, also attended by government officials. She noticed a disused pump on the other side of the village. "What is that?" she asked. A village elder replied, "Ah, that is the other water pump! The driller came and installed it, but after a while, it broke and nobody knew how to fix it. So the government said they will build another one."

In this case, the plan was sensible on paper and all the correct steps were followed, but cultural factors were not taken into account. The community did not directly state its needs (to fix the broken pump), the NGO did not conduct a deep analysis to avoid wasting resources on an expensive project and the government took the opportunity to boost its prestige by obtaining a shiny thing for the community and basking in the positive press.

The Power of Relationships

In a social culture like Ghana, relationships are critical: it is not what you know but who you know. Hard skills will get you far with logistical planning, construction and product development, but the soft skills will ensure the success of your operations. Even if you have an excellent operation and a strong team, forces outside of your organization and control can bring it to its knees.

Relationships are what get things done – the aforementioned "golden key". When a key deliverable or approval is being held up in bureaucracy, a phone call to the right person can resolve the issue, clearing the blockage. However, it is more than just knowing people, but also about establishing and cultivating relationships and strategically leveraging them. Doing this effectively will require all of your intercultural effectiveness with Ghanaians. This section will look further at how to do business with Ghanaians.

Greetings

Effective communication starts with greetings. For Ghanaians, greetings are not typically brief and perfunctory; they are rituals that reinforce the social, harmonious and hierarchical nature of the culture and are not to be hurried. Skipping these to "get down to business" is viewed as rude.

If you are meeting a group, try to shake hands from right to left, always using the right hand. Do not be too firm in your handshake. Once you know a person, you can use the Ghanaian handshake that ends in a mutual finger-snap[76], particularly with men. Handshakes

---

[76] This is worth practicing, even if unable to snap one's fingers. Also, if you meet a Ghanaian outside of Ghana, greeting with "the snap" is a great way to immediately make an impression on them.

can last throughout the greeting process. If your hand is not clean, place it over your heart in greeting.

When engaging in any communication with a Ghanaian, always greet, even if to ask for directions, or if passing by on the street. When interrupting to engage someone, greet the person you are interrupting. When greeting someone familiar, start with "How are you?" then ask about their health, their family and any other pertinent information (their travels, their business). In this way, greeting a person or group may last well over a minute.

To break the ice, you can divulge your Akan name[77], which is often good for a smile and demonstrates your familiarity. For men, be sure to introduce female colleagues and demonstrate that they are your equals.

Meetings

If arranging a meeting with public official or businessperson, you may need to provide a formal request in writing. You may also need to follow-up with your desired interlocutor, including confirmation by phone (or if your calls are not answered, identifying yourself by text). Working through assistants can be frustrating, so either cultivate a good relationship with them, or go straight to the Big Man/Woman. Once set, call again to confirm closer to the date, which will also remind the person of the meeting's importance in the face of competing priorities.

Group meetings in Ghana are formal, regularly with a set agenda, a chair and a minute-taker. However, start times are often subject to

---

[77] Recall from Cultural Rituals: Weddings, Outdoorings and Funerals that Akan first names are based on the gender and day of the week of their birth. Also, for males born on Sunday (Kwesi), know that *Kwesi 'Bruni* is slang for a white guy, like "Joe six-pack".

GMT and may be out of your control, particularly if a Big Man/Woman is expected. Meetings can also go well beyond their set end time as all items need to be raised and discussed by all participants. Hierarchy is observed throughout. Address your interlocutors first by title (e.g. Doctor, Chief Director, Minister) and last name until you are familiar. Remember to start with small talk, getting to know each other before getting down to business. They may be familiar with or have even visited your home country, which makes for good initial small talk.

Organizing a lunch meeting can be a good idea, particularly when discussing a challenging issue or trying to attract a full team. While meetings can be for equals, it can lead to power imbalances in relationships – for example, if a counterpart brings an entourage to lunch. A meal at an upscale restaurant or hotel is almost never required – a mid-range restaurant or catering at the office boardroom will do just as well and for far less. Unless your counterpart has a particular restaurant preference, Ghanaian or Chinese cuisine is the safest choice. Remember that whether for lunch, dinner or drinks, the person who invites is expected to pay.

Whether dining with your own team, colleagues, potential clients or government officials, a quick shortcut to building rapport and gaining respect is to go Ghanaian. Foreigners are not known for their love of Ghanaian cuisine. Get to know the food and how to eat it. While jollof and chicken is an easy route, learn how to take fufu with your hands like a local. In Ghanaian culture, food is a communal experience, from pouring water over each other's hands prior to eating, to sharing a bowl of soup.

Speeches and Presentations

Diplomats and persons in leadership positions may find themselves giving speeches. First, to respect hierarchy, ensure that you acknowledge the dignitaries, concluding with the phrase "all protocol observed". Check with a trusted local colleague to confirm who is in the audience and will merit an acknowledgement and in what order.

You may open with a few words in the local language of the area. In your speech, you can use some light humour, which will be appreciated, but may not always translate well. You can make positive references to Ghanaian democracy; the economy; social harmony; hospitality; the national football team, the Black Stars; Ghana's historical role in the African independence movement as well as positive differences between Ghanaians and Nigerians. Avoid sensitive issues, including ethnic differences, corruption, crime, religion or political issues (particularly avoiding any perceived preference for either of the two main political parties, NDC and NPP).

Speak slowly, as all foreign accents can be difficult to understand. English is often the second language of Ghanaians and the command depends on the person's background. Try to lower your pitch – there is a playful stereotype of obruni women with high-pitched voices. Project your voice, particularly when acoustics can be poor. If your audience is falling asleep, liven the room up.

Be conscious of time: speeches can go on at great length and you could be one of several speakers on the schedule. Brevity can be memorable.

If giving a presentation, note that PowerPoint is regularly used, but as in other countries, it is typically done with little finesse. Often, slides are full of text and read verbatim, including financial tables.

An effective presentation can also be memorable and save valuable meeting time.

Your audience may seem disinterested and not all may pay attention, including answering phone calls[78]. If you are not sure, you can call out to the audience for their acknowledgement by asking, "Do you get me?" Participants may look to leaders to provide responses. However, the Q&A session can be lively, with long and lively interjections.

Regardless, asking questions for clarification in a group setting is not common in Ghanaian culture, as the person would often feel embarrassed to be seen as unknowledgeable[79]. In this case, a person may bring a genuine question to you privately afterwards.

Workshops, Training and Conferences

For workshops, training and conferences, manage your time and that of others: set the ground rules and ask the room how they would like to proceed, especially if running late. People may be eager to get home. Lunch is typically a full hour. Keep an eye on Ramadan, particularly in the North, as Muslim participants would have to forego lunch and snacks and possibly appreciate an early end time. Allow prayer time during breaks.

Conference location matters, especially for government staff. A conference may not be taken seriously if it is not at a relatively prestigious location, such as a hotel. Particularly attractive for bureaucrats are locations outside of the Greater Accra Region like

---

[78] This happens for a good reason: if a Ghanaian caller cannot reach their contact, they often will call repeatedly until the phone is answered.

[79] This starts in school, where teachers traditionally lecture commandingly and students learn by rote, focusing on memorization of facts rather than inquiry and discussion.

Koforidua and Dodowa, which allow public servants to request per diems ("T&T") from their employer. Offering per diems to invitees or at least a transportation allowance can help to encourage their participation[80].

Before an event, think through the required logistics. E-mail your presentation to yourself and prepare a thumb drive. Ask ahead for printouts and copies if needed. Services may not be available on-site, but can be secured.

Learning the Language

When discussing business, language matters. Potential business partners and government officials may speak the Queen's English better than you. However, working-class Ghanaians may use more fluid pidgin English that can take some time for a foreigner to understand. In rural areas, English may be used rarely as a second (or third) language. Ghanaians are proud of their respective languages and English comes second. If you are not certain, use simplified language to communicate your thoughts clearly and concisely. Avoid your culture's idioms, but learn about Ghanaian slang and local terms. It is helpful to know that a rubber sandal is a *chale wote*, that *dumsor* means a power outage and *chop* means street food – but the verb *to chop* is to embezzle money[81].

Inversely, the Ghanaian command of English can be excellent, with a masterful use of formal and descriptive language. When exiting a trotro, a Ghanaian *alights*. When closing correspondence, a Ghanaian

---

[80] Per diem rates are unregulated for non-bureaucrats and context-specific. There is a perennial debate among internationals in Ghana on whether paying people to attend events is a good use of funds, or if it fosters a market for workshop participants. However, it may be a necessary evil to attract participants.

[81] More slang can be found in Michael Kponor's *Ghana's Best Guide to Pidgin English*.

ends *Please be assured of our highest compliments.* When texted by an unknown number, a Ghanaian replies *By His Grace, who is this?* Read a newspaper article or listen to a lecturer to get a sense of the vocabulary of Ghanaians[82]. Over time, you will get a feel for this approach to the language and it will become natural as saying *No condition is permanent!*

As with many working cultures, acronyms are prized and used regularly, particularly with organizations and programs. Do not be afraid to ask for clarification on the meaning. For example, MoGCSP (pronounced "MOG-ship") is the Ministry of Gender, Children and Social Protection.

Working with Government and Bureaucracy

From the moment one steps into the customs line at the airport, they will encounter the Ghanaian bureaucracy. The government, while unable to effectively provide many basic services, has the market cornered on policies, processes and approvals. Many of these appear straightforward on paper, but anyone who has tried to obtain a service, from a visa to a vehicle license knows that there is always a complication – something missing or an additional step, approval or fee. Time matters little to public servants, who have excellent job security and little accountability.

The bureaucracy is a complex machine and many foreigners have tried to avoid it, best it or reform it, yet it remains. Rarely does one have leverage. In this case, how you approach a bureaucrat determines how they will react. A respectful and polite attitude may

---

[82] Business guides will warn the reader to avoid pretentious, formal, stylish or inflated language, which is seen as unnecessarily long, complex and showy. However, this presents a western style of thinking. In Ghana, formality matters, as does taking the time to make one's point. What would seem direct and effective in your country might be seen as foreign and aggressive to Ghanaians.

or may not expedite things, but an aggressive or angry one will guarantee that your desired goal will take longer than it should. Try to humanize yourself so that you are seen as a person and not a problem. Ask specific questions that clarify the process. Be aware that delays may be for reasons ranging from the mundane (such as when the office printer is broken) to the opportune. Often an additional fee could expedite the process, but this is not recommended for two reasons: 1) it is not guaranteed to work, and 2) if it does work, it can contribute to a marketplace where payment is the new standard for service.

Many organizations with recurring needs will employ Ghanaians who know how to work the bureaucracy, either as a property manager or a specialist in their field. What better person to obtain a vehicle permit than an experienced driver or reliable electricity connections than the electrician? They are more likely to have the patience, discretion and skills to navigate the bureaucracy.

Decision-making in Ghanaian culture is hierarchical, so a person at the front desk may not even have the authority to approve. Further up the chain is where the big decisions are made: the Big Men and Women. Depending on your work, you may have interaction with people in power, including the head of a municipal assembly or district (the mayor/district chief executive), a ministry's top public servant (the chief director) or the responsible minister, who may be an elected member of parliament or an appointee. Do your homework on the leadership structure of the organization and discern who makes the real decisions.

Gift, Dash or Bribe?

As discussed in Managing and Leading Ghanaians, one can address corruption within their own organization, but what about when working with others, particularly when things need to be done quickly and efficiently? Every organization will have to make a decision at some point on how to address the issue of corruption. However, corruption takes many forms and it is not black-and-white but many different shades of gray.

What is the difference between a gift, a dash and a bribe?

Gift-giving is traditional in Ghanaian culture and it is an important ritual that strengthens social connections, gives respect and maintains harmony. Historically, when one returned from a long journey, they would bring something home for family and friends[83]. When seeking an audience with a chief, one brings alcohol or kola nuts. In rural areas, a gift of yams or a live chicken or guinea fowl is still common. Ghanaians give monetary gifts regularly, whether for weddings, funerals, church collections or needy relatives needing help with basic needs, including hospital and school fees. Those higher on the wealth ladder are expected to help those with less.

Gift-giving is rarely appreciated as a practice by foreigners, who may either not have been raised in a gift-giving culture, or whose organizational culture discourages or strictly forbids it. Consequently, foreigners are seen by Ghanaians as stingy. To reinforce social bonds, small gifts can make a large difference to Ghanaians (or in the case of weddings and funerals, large ones). Inversely, when a foreigner is offered a gift by a community after providing development assistance, it is part of a ritual and it may be difficult to refuse. The farmer who offers part of his or her crop is not depriving him or herself of a meager possession, but is honouring you as a guest. So think twice before refusing it, as it could be a major faux pas[84].

---

[83] Recall that on return from travels, friends and colleagues will ask, "What did you bring me?" The value of the gift is irrelevant, but it affirms your social bonds. Chocolates or candy is a safe bet.

[84] As a compromise that maintains harmony, one can take a small part of the gift

Working with Ghanaians

A dash can be a few things. As noted, it can be a token of gratitude from a street vendor after completing a deal. It can also be a small tip for servers, attendants or people known to have a very meager income. However, it can also be given to a police officer at a roadblock in place of a more serious discussion, search or possible ticket[85]. Occasionally, a snack or bottle of water can pass for a friendly gift, but an officer fishing for a full-on bribe may quickly become the stereotypical "bad cop" and if your papers are not in order, decisions will become more difficult.

When a gift is given in expectation of a favour in the future, it becomes a bribe. When a gift is given in thanks of a service provided, it can be perceived as a quid pro quo. Anything that calls into question the integrity of a system can be a problem, whether it is a real, apparent or potential conflict of interest.

As a foreigner with resources or diplomatic credentials, who you associate with matters. Ghanaians tend to "know" who is honest and who is corrupt. When they see foreigners associating with people perceived as corrupt (politicians, high rollers), they will make judgments on you and your character. One foreigner's advice: beware the man who drives a Highlander.

Foreign and Ghanaian professionals have varying opinions on how to deal with corruption. Some say that it is inevitable from the bottom to the top and is simply a business expense that can only be minimized as best as possible. Small firms can be particularly affected: the cost of delays of goods at the port can be far greater than the payment required to the clearing agent to facilitate its processing.

---

offered, like a single yam, as a symbol that the gift has been accepted.

[85] Officers seem to never have pads of tickets but are always happy to settle on the spot rather than taking a drive down to the police station to process you.

However, paying bribes tends to stimulate the marketplace and make it harder for the next person. This explains the *goro boys*[86] hanging out at the Driver and Vehicle Licensing Authority and even the Ghana Revenue Authority during tax season. Even more frustrating than paying a bribe is paying it to the wrong person and getting no results from it. Not all demands are serious, but it can be difficult to differentiate a threat from a bluff. Once you are in someone's pocket, it is difficult to get out.

On the other hand, companies find ways around outright bribery and can sometimes find a mutually-agreeable solution by sponsoring an event, leading a public awareness campaign or contributing to a charitable cause[87].

There is always a way of doing the right thing. If you insist on the right thing to be done, it might be hard and frustrating, but you will prevail and will come out satisfied. Some may think that a foreigner is an easy source of cash, but if you work the system well and demonstrate your integrity, people will respect you.

"A good name is better than riches."
-Proverbs 22.1 (and an honorary Ghanaian proverb)

---

[86] Goro boys are middlemen who facilitate public services with government, to put it charitably.
[87] Recall the opportunity to make deals in Negotiation.

Vignette #3: Kumasi, Ashanti Region

I took an unforgettable trip to Kumasi to watch the Ghanaian national men's football team qualify for the World Cup. After the match, I stayed with a friend working at a local startup, a mixed team of Ghanaian and international coders living and working together at a house near the Kwame Nkrumah University of Science and Technology. Unlike most offices, this had a flat organizational structure, strong cross-cultural bonds and a shared team culture. In fact, it was almost like a family.

Arthur was a coder hired out of school who had wisdom beyond his years. I asked him: what is in the secret sauce here? He replied that the problems the startup wanted to solve needed open-minded people and a collaborative culture. The team worked together, gave everyone a voice and reviewed and shared feedback regularly. Rather than directing workers like soldiers, managers asked the question: "How can I support you to do what you want to do?"

Arthur's scrappy startup has grown beyond the campus: it now is headquartered in an office in Accra and has over 200 staff in 35 countries around the world. Yet the company's culture remains dynamic and inclusive, showing a different way to manage a Ghanaian company.

Working with Ghanaians

Building Bridges

A diplomat, after several years in Ghana, left the country dissatisfied. She had been briefed that Ghanaians were notoriously friendly, yet found herself making friends only with her fellow foreigners. She remarked near the end of her time that in her home country, a new colleague from abroad would be immediately welcomed and invited to a household feast. In four years, she had never seen the inside of a Ghanaian colleague's house and took this as a personal slight. Another diplomat had spent four years and worked hard to build bridges and understand Ghanaians, fostering strong working relations. At her departure, an expat-Ghanaian party was held in her honour, attended by three ministers. Years later, Ghanaians still ask after her.

On the face of it, making these connections seems easy: Ghanaians are social and make fast friends, striking up conversations with neighbours on trotros, buses or planes and exchanging phone numbers with ease. Foreigners who stand out in the crowd will make many friends even more quickly.

Those who do share their phone number will regularly receive calls and texts from their new friends, often simply to say hello, but sometimes to ask for assistance.

At the office, harmony is the standard and so Ghanaian colleagues and employees will warmly greet you, asking after your family and engaging easily in chit-chat. This can evolve into deep discussions with colleagues on politics, the economy, religion and other weighty matters. From outward appearances, you are becoming fast friends.

Many Friends on Paper

In spite of this, foreigners may find it difficult to foster deep reciprocal friendships with Ghanaians. Many leave Ghana after several years counting only a handful of people among close friends (including their househelp). Foreigners with genuinely good intentions and efforts have found themselves unable to cultivate the deep friendships that they would expect arising from time spent in other cultures.

Ghanaian culture, while primarily a social, communal and harmonious one, is in its own way insular to outsiders. Ghanaian culture is very strong and complex with many layers and so one cannot easily insert themselves into it. There are a few reasons for this:

If you are coming to Ghana on contract or assignment for a short period (several months to a few years), you are impermanent. Deep relationships are fostered over time, which may not always be possible in the time of your contract.

As a professional, whether you like it or not, you are part of the hierarchy. In the communal Ghanaian culture, remember that those with much are expected to do their share for others. It may seem that people are always expecting you to help them with their financial, employment or visa problems. This can lead to a sense of isolation. Much like the wealthy and celebrities, foreigners find themselves with few people they feel they can connect with and trust.

Even within one's own class and profession, foreigners have difficulty making Ghanaian friends. Highly successful Ghanaians often have different interests, including supporting large families, managing multiple business or social ventures and would rather spend a weekend in London than on the beach in Takoradi. Their networks may be based on their families, church or alumni networks.

Ghanaian colleagues also may feel intimidated by you. If invited out for dinner and drinks, could they afford the meal? Could they keep up with you if you decided to go to a lounge afterwards? It would be an extravagant expenditure for people supporting a family and counting their cedis. Likewise, you could easily invite a Ghanaian into your house, but would they feel comfortable inviting you? They may feel that they would need to roll out the red carpet and buy expensive food and drink. And what would you think of their house without air conditioning or a generator? So there may be a tangential reason for keeping an arms-length friendship.

You may be keen to make friends with Ghanaians, while doing the wrong things: foreigners like to spend Sunday by the pool, enjoying brunch with friends or perhaps engaging in a recreational activity, like cycling, hiking or tennis. Most Ghanaians spend Sunday at church and with family, perhaps with an occasional visit to the beach.

The unfortunate reality is that you cannot make close friends with everyone. Your means, interests and values are different from those of most Ghanaians. There is a gap between the cultures of Ghanaians and foreigners. However, in this case, the cultural icebergs are touching beneath the surface, with common interests. Some of these interests are very casual and transactional, but if you can go deep enough, some can get to the core of one's identity and lead to meaningful relationships.

Ways to Build Bridges

The following are some ideas for meeting Ghanaians, building networks and casual friendships and cultivating deeper ones as well, including with colleagues and clients. Remember that even the most interculturally effective people will have to work at this.

Easy Things

There are many things that one can do that require little effort, touching the visible part of the iceberg. The first is to concretely demonstrate your openness to and appreciation of Ghanaian culture. Start with finding some Friday wear. A trip to the market and to find a tailor/seamstress is itself a cultural experience. For women, consider picking up some Ghanaian beadwork. Look for authentic made-in-Ghana wax print or batik fabric and glass beads if possible (there are plenty of cheap imported knock-offs). In whatever case, find something that works for you and then find more. Buying and wearing Ghanaian will earn respect and as you will see, proud Ghanaians wear their culture any day of the week.

Food is another visible symbol of Ghanaian culture. Many foreigners find Ghanaian food adventurous and daunting, but with a bit of browsing, one can find the things that appeal most to them. For many, their standard Ghanaian meal is chicken and jollof rice – almost every restaurant serves it. Ask a friend or colleague where they can find the best jollof and if you could take them out to lunch to try. Tilapia is the other standard protein.

Ghanaians are particularly proud of their food and few stray far from it. There are many restaurants serving Italian, Lebanese or Indian cuisine, but these are mostly for foreigners and well-traveled Ghanaians. However, if you want to have lunch or dinner with a friend or colleague and want to go international, there are a few options. Chinese food is popular for Ghanaians. Few fast food chains have managed to crack the Ghanaian market, but the exception is Kentucky Fried Chicken, which has cracked the Ghanaian middle class. A bucket of KFC with fries or rice is enjoyed equally by foreigners and Ghanaians of all stripes and makes an easy team lunch or treat for a friend.

Ghana's music scene is vibrant, from old-school highlife and afrobeat legends to chart-topping hiplife, dancehall and azonto artists. There is a great deal of live music to enjoy and colleagues and friends can give their recommendations.

Following Ghanaian current events is another easy way to connect with Ghanaians. The Ghanaian media is quite vibrant, with print and web outlets. While some cultures discourage discussion of politics, almost every Ghanaian has an opinion on the government or the opposition and lively debate is the norm. It may take time to separate fact from opinion, speculation and fiction, but knowing the domestic political situation will help you to better understand the country. Social media can provide additional context to issues by observing commentators and citizen opinions on the matters.

A natural way to connect, particularly with Ghanaian men, is football. Ghana has made multiple trips to the World Cup and counts many Ghanaians in first-tier leagues worldwide. Ghanaian men follow the English Premier League and Champions League in particular, with matches broadcast on national television. There is also a Ghanaian Premier League with strong rivalries, particularly between Accra Hearts of Oak and Kumasi's Asante Kotoko. Ask a Ghanaian man who is their preferred English team or about the Black Stars' chances at the next African Cup of Nations. If you fancy yourself a good player, see if you can join an informal game – many happen early Sunday morning before church.

There are also mixed sports groups like the Accra Hash, Ghana's chapter of the Hash House Harriers international network. This intercultural group meets weekly for a group run through various neighbourhoods of Accra and Tema, followed by drinks and some peculiar but light-hearted rituals (it is popularly known as a "drinking club with a running problem").

Not-So-Easy Things

In Ghana, you can get by anywhere with English. In spite of this, there are secondary common languages, from Twi to pidgin. Learning the local language is not always possible, but depending on where you are, consider trying to learn the basics of the language, including greetings, expressions, common words and Akan names. Ghanaians are amused, impressed and flattered when a foreigner uses their language and are less likely to brush you off as just another obruni. It may take some effort to master even basic pronunciation, but you will earn respect. You may also find that it opens doors into unexpected areas in building relationships and in negotiations.

On food, while jollof and chicken is an easy route, Ghanaian cuisine goes much deeper and few experience it. There are the mashes of fufu, banku, kenkey and tuo zafi; stews like groundnut, light soup and okro; proteins like guinea fowl and grasscutter; and snacks like suya kebabs, plantain chips, wagashi cheese and FanIce. Foreigners try few of these, but those who acquire the taste have a far better experience – especially when on the road.

In Ghanaian culture, food is a communal experience, from pouring water over each other's hands prior to eating, to sharing a bowl of soup. Ghanaians often assume that foreigners will not eat their food. This may be another reason why they are hesitant to invite you to their house. However, if you learn how to take fufu like a Ghanaian, you are more likely to be treated seriously by colleagues, employees and potential clients. In addition, if you are in a rural area, your options may be limited or you may be offered one meal and refusing it would be an insult to your host.

Ghanaian culture values its meat and fish, so this may be particularly difficult for vegetarians or vegans who regularly need to explain themselves politely to their confused hosts. However, there are Ghanaian meals without meat and fish, like waakye, gari foto and tatale. Chinese food may be a good compromise, as tofu dishes can be eaten alongside meat dishes.

A bonus activity is to engage in cross-cultural culinary education by learning how to make a favourite dish. Offer to host an informal lesson or see if the colleague is willing to host you at their house[88].

Hard Things

Deeply integrating into Ghanaian society requires a lot of time and effort, engaging Ghanaians on their own terms and openness to an entirely different way of thinking.

For the religious, church and mosque are common bonds. Joining a church and participating regularly is one way to make friends. Finding the right church may be challenging as foreigners may find even their denomination to be much different in Ghana, where mainline churches feature lively music and pastors preaching call-and-response to their parishioners. So why not take advantage of this liveliness and join the church choir or band? Volunteering is also an area where one can find like-minded Ghanaians, which can include faith-based organizations.

If you have children in school, you may find like-minded parents at school performances, parent-teacher associations or even at children's birthday parties, which often have a table for parents to congregate with food and drink.

The academic world features opportunities to meet professional Ghanaians. The University of Ghana at Legon and to a lesser extent Kwame Nkrumah University of Science and Technology in Kumasi

---

[88] Recall that some colleagues may be hesitant to host you at their house for reasons of pride, so insist that you would prefer to learn in an authentic Ghanaian kitchen, but do not press if they seem uncomfortable.

have international student programs and are connected to international networks of researchers. Ashesi University near Aburi has recently established itself as a high-quality liberal arts school with a mixed Ghanaian-international staff and student body.

In addition, there are thousands of foreigners married to Ghanaians and who have integrated into Ghanaian culture, so it is possible! Indeed, many of these people came to Ghana to work and have fallen in love with Ghanaians.

A Few Shortcuts

Ghanaians being social, have taken to social media, but often have particular networks and ways of using them. For example, while Facebook is globally predominant and many Ghanaians have an account, WhatsApp has become the way to communicate, including international calling, texting, group discussions, posting event notices and sharing news (real and imagined), rumours, jokes and memes. Twitter, Instagram and other platforms also are useful for finding out about events and trends. Find out what your friends and colleagues are on and start communicating on the network.

Ghana's youth are highly tech savvy and plugged into online social networks. The arts and technology scenes in particular feature open-minded and adventurous university students and graduates. Accra and Kumasi are tech hubs, with entrepreneurs and social groups trying new and exciting things.

Visual and musical artists are also found all over. Jamestown's Chale Wote festival held every August has grown into a massive event, attracting tens of thousands of Ghanaians and plenty of adventurous foreigners. It features performance art, workshops and other networking opportunities. With the number of live music venues, bringing an instrument along is a good idea.

Working with Ghanaians

There are shortcuts, but overall, you will need to take a long-term approach to forming, developing and benefiting from relationships with Ghanaians. Building bridges with Ghanaians and building deep, meaningful relationships takes time and effort and it may or may not turn out the way you expect it. However, those who can develop them will yield benefits: gaining new friendships, a wider network and even an improved quality of life, feeling less stressed and more at home in Ghana.

Little by little, little by little, as we drink we make plans.
-Akan proverb

Working with Ghanaians

Afterword: Ezekiel's Haircut

Recently I was in my hometown and had just received a haircut at a local salon. As I was paying the bill, a young African man came in. He seemed quite unsure of whether he was in the right place. He did not speak much English (and no French) inquired awkwardly if the hairdressers could cut "black" hair, as the staff and clientele was white. The hairdresser confirmed that they can and asked if he would like a fade or razor, but he was not quite sure what she meant. She also was becoming unsure of herself and was even having difficulty recording his name, Ezekiel – a common Biblical name.

The situation seemed a bit odd, but as the neighbourhood is ethnically diverse, I thought it would end up fine and it was not my business to intrude in a private matter. After exiting, it dawned upon me that there was a serious intercultural misunderstanding and that I should have used my own intercultural skills learned with Ghanaians. I should have welcomed him, asked where he was from and asked more questions about what he wanted. African barbers often have photos. Did he have an example to show, like an old selfie on his phone? I decided to check back in, but by then he had departed. It was a missed opportunity to bridge a cultural gap.

I should have immediately understood this, as I have lived this awkward experience many times in Ghana and elsewhere in Africa and I know how frustrating and disheartening it can be. The lesson here could be that intercultural effectiveness can be used wherever in the world you travel, but it can also be a continuing challenge that takes regular effort and self-awareness. I hope Ezekiel found what he was looking for and I hope that the next time I meet him, I will be as helpful as a Ghanaian would be to me.

Working with Ghanaians

Annex: Working With...

This book has discussed working with Ghanaians inside and outside of the office, but for simplicity's sake has not discussed particular professions in depth. Foreigners are likely to work with or manage Ghanaians working in the professions discussed below. Note that for employment, salaries are almost always negotiable, so when deciding on an amount, do your homework and ask around for a sense of the market rate.

Cleaners

Things need to be cleaned often in Ghana. Humidity brings mold and food rots quickly. Harmattan winds bring dust on floors, cars and clothes. Cleaning the home and office is labour-intensive in Ghana. For most foreigners, time is money and labour is relatively cheap. So hiring a cleaner is an attractive choice, whether full-time or part-time.

As jobs go for Ghanaians, cleaning for foreigners is a relatively desirable job: relatively light manual labour, reasonable hours, and no serious education required.

Finding someone willing to clean is easy, but finding the appropriate person is more challenging. A cleaner should be literate, especially when expected to handle serious cleaning products. Provide clear direction on expectations with tasks and materials and demonstrate your preferred method. Some will mop with litres of antiseptic solution while others will spend the day pushing around the same cloudy water. A weekly schedule is recommended to ensure that no task is left undone.

Cooks and Caterers

This is another job that attracts a diverse group of people and has no set standard. For Ghanaians, a caterer is anyone who can make the local staples and has the equipment to do it. Caterers often work in teams, so budget accordingly.

For non-Ghanaian food, a good cook will be able to take a recipe and figure it out with some guidance and trial-and-error. Clever ones will know where to substitute when ingredients are scarce. Ghanaians are used to eating a fairly standard set of meals, so cooks may rely on a few favourites at the expense of genuine variety. However, plenty of feedback will ensure that the cook knows what is going well and what is not. If a good rapport is established, it will be possible to discuss performance and get feedback as well. The view from inside the kitchen is often a fascinating one and much can be learned about colleagues by their ordering and eating habits.

Househelp

"Househelp" is a general term in Ghana for a domestic worker. It can include cooking, cleaning, gardening, minding children, and even supervising deliveries or handymen. Managing househelp would be a book in itself. However, there are a few key things to know particular:

First and foremost, househelp are employees. They happen to work in the house with the family and over time can become quite close, but nevertheless remain employees. This distinction normally blurs over time and househelp often become like family to the employer. This is amplified with live-in househelp who are around almost 24/7. Regardless, ensure that the househelp is employed via a contract that can be understood by all parties. Start with a probationary period to determine suitability. If the househelp requests a loan, garnish the salary accordingly and demand collateral if needed (see: Money Matters). Also ensure that the househelp receives an employer contribution for the National Health Insurance Scheme (NHIS) and the legally-required Social Security and National Insurance Trust (SSNIT). Just as important is to ensure that the househelp is registered and makes the required payments, which may require a day's leave and can be confirmed with an invoice. Otherwise, you may find yourself being begged to pay the househelp's out-of-pocket expenses in an emergency. Additional benefits can be negotiated (e.g. immunizations, allowance for commuting).

Househelp is another job that by Ghanaian standards is relatively light labour, requiring not too much education. It also is a role traditionally filled by women and girls. There is a perceived hierarchy of preferred employers for househelp, which may or may not reflect reality. Western expats are often at the top of the list: conscious of the rights of the employee[89], they generally demand lower hours, less tasks and pay the most livable wages. Next are Indians and Lebanese. Their requirements are seen as much stricter, demanding and offering lower salaries. Lower still are Chinese. At the bottom are Ghanaians. Domestic servitude has been practiced in one form or another in Ghana for centuries, so having a "house girl" or "house boy" is not unusual, including employing a relative. The hierarchy in society applies to the house. The long hours and low wages are reflective of an average job in Ghana.

There are professional cleaning services and human resources agencies with househelp rosters. However, the most common way to hire househelp is still via personal networks and word-of-mouth.

---

[89] Western expats are also less likely to have employed househelp before. Consequently, they may be less demanding or at least more uncertain of what is a reasonable workload or tasking for househelp.

Given the level of trust in househelp, personal recommendations and references are very important. Even on social media pages, departing expats post advertisements on behalf of their househelp or those of friends. Expats may even feel an implied duty and sense of obligation to assist the househelp with onward employment. This is also important as househelp rarely keep résumés or letters of reference.

Househelp often have access to most of the employer's house and belongings. For this reason, security is paramount. It is important to have a space that is off-limits to protect money, key documents and valuables. A safe is recommended.

Most importantly, if you do not feel that you can trust your househelp, do not put them in a position of trust. Unfortunately, burglaries and home invasions do occur and disgruntled househelp are a common cause. However, househelp can also be compromised, including via threats to them or their family. Even with iron bars and reinforced locks, a person with a key can access any lock. For this reason, having a "safe room" with a separate keylock is recommended.

If you decide to dismiss househelp, do so immediately. Demand any keys provided and issue the agreed-upon severance pay. If the househelp is live-in, agree on a reasonable move-out date. Finding affordable space in the city is quite difficult, but be firm. Removing an obstinate tenant can be quite challenging.

Gardeners

In a country as green as Ghana, houses, compounds and offices often have relatively elaborate and well-manicured grounds. Unless one misses the thrill of watering and weeding a garden or mowing the grass, a gardener is a helpful option for keeping the grounds tidy.

Gardeners tend to be male and on the lower end of the educational spectrum. Like anyone executing another's ideas, gardeners know what they know and don't know what they don't know. So if you have a firm idea of what you would like in your grounds, make it known and discuss how to achieve the desired end. The same goes for maintenance. If you would like to restrict water usage during the dry season (for environmental or practical reasons) let it be known. Also, figure out a budget for plants, tools and mower (including fuel). Finally, if you want particular plants in your grounds, you may need to search for them yourself, as plant variety and quality in Ghana differ from other places with similar climates, like Southeast Asia and the Caribbean.

Mechanics

"A good name is better than riches," goes a Ghanaian proverb on the importance of integrity. Anywhere in the world, this could also apply to mechanics. The same goes in Ghana. Ask for the name of a trusted mechanic. A good mechanic can check a car before it is purchased, provides quality service for the owner and even roadside assistance.

If buying a car, an inspection of a third-party can confirm the general condition of the car, what parts will need replacement, and if the seller is being honest (perhaps that SUV is not really a 4-wheel drive as advertised).

In developed countries, labour is expensive, while parts are plentiful and cheap, so mechanics are engaged sparingly and parts are simply replaced. In Ghana, labour is quite cheap, while parts are scarce and expensive – particularly for uncommon makes and models, like North American brands. Thus, mechanics often will fix a broken part over the course of a day at a reasonable cost to the owner. In addition, a good mechanic will come to your home or office to pick up the vehicle and return it as well.

Quality is often an issue, so get your work checked if needed. Quick fixes may ignore larger issues or lead to additional ones. Fraud is also possible: a second look led to one foreigner finding out that his colleague's "reliable" mechanic was conducting non-existent air conditioning repair and charging the company for the work.

As for roadside assistance, if your vehicle breaks down, your mechanic should be able to send someone to investigate and call a tow truck if needed. There is no Ghana Automobile Association. However, in Accra there is an army of ancient-but-trusty Land Rover tow trucks throughout the city.

Most car brands have an authorized dealer in Accra that provides maintenance, including from cars recently purchased from them, which makes them an attractive option for foreign companies. There is a premium attached to this and – crucially – you may have to bring the car to them in Accra traffic.

Handymen

As Ghana has a rather harsh climate coupled with no maintenance culture, things break down, including plumbing, electricity, air conditioners, generators and many other items. Enter the handyman (unfortunately, still mostly men). As with mechanics, good ones are worth keeping around.

A common feature of handymen in Ghana is that they rarely carry their own tools. Often, when responding to a house call, the handyman will look at the malfunctioning appliance, state that they do not have the correct tool to fix it, then drive back to the workshop to obtain it. So having a full toolbox (screwdrivers, wrenches, measuring tape and hammer) and a decent flashlight can skip this step and save a half-day's waiting.

The training and experience of handymen varies. Where you have an issue, clearly communicate the challenge as best you can. Afterwards, check the work before they depart to ensure that 1) you are satisfied with the work, 2) the item in question is back in order, and 3) no additional problems have been created. For larger tasks, ensuring that the workers have water and providing some chop will buy goodwill.

Servers and Sales Associates

As noted in Understanding Ghanaians, there is a particular service culture in Ghana that can leave some foreigners feeling frustrated. Recall that for Ghanaians, servers are seeking harmony to please their customers, while also providing the appropriate deference and hierarchical respect.

Ghanaian patrons are more likely to be short and sharp with their servers in what expats would consider a brusque manner ("Bring me this") and show less courtesy, being the one served.

With sales associates, ensure that they accord you adequate attention and respect. If you are looking for something in particular, describe it clearly. If the store does not carry precisely what you want, the server may be disappointed in a potential lost sale or frustrated in the customer who may seem too picky.

A similar approach may work with restaurants. Often, a server might casually take a meal order and not relay it precisely to the cook, providing something different than what was expected, frustrating the patron. It helps to be clear when you order and to ask the server to repeat what was heard, to confirm that the message was received –

check as many times as needed and stay calm. If an order is slow to come, you will be told "please, it's coming", but you can ask for more precision on when and you can also indicate when a wait is becoming unreasonable. Afterwards, give a modest (not a percentage-based) tip for service. Let managers know when their servers and associates are doing good work.

When employing servers and sales associates, some training and coaching may be required. While foreigners find Ghanaian customer service strange, many Ghanaians find western customer service alien as well, though urban, media-savvy and well-travelled Ghanaians may be more attuned to this perspective. The bottom line is that if you wish to instill a particular service mentality into a server or sales associate, it may require some time to discuss who the customer is, what the customer wants and how to effectively address the customer's needs (e.g. a customer may *want* a meal, but has a *need* to feel respected and appreciated), as well as feedback and review.

Tailors and Seamstresses

While malls and clothing stores are on the rise in Accra and second-hand clothing stalls are found throughout the country[90], Ghana is famous for its bright and high-quality fabrics. Ghana also has its share of fashion-forward and world-renowned designers. With the low cost of labour, one can easily produce (or reproduce) custom-made clothing for less than what they would pay for clothes in a store in one's home country. Repairs are also quite reasonable.

---

[90] There is a major international trade in second-hand clothing, with the bulk of items coming from donations to charity shops, which sell their excess clothing in wholesale bundles for export worldwide. In Ghana, this is known as *obruni wawu*, or "dead man's clothing" and has both taken over local markets and sharply reduced demand for tailors and seamstresses as well as locally-produced textiles.

Working with Ghanaians

Tailors and seamstresses abound in Ghana. Usually tailors produce for men and seamstresses for women, but this is not always the case. Skill and quality vary greatly, so it may require some trial-and-error to find the right person for you. Do you want them to shop for you, or simply make clothing based on what you have purchased in the market[91]? When designing Friday wear or something more formal, be very precise with your needs. Multiple meetings with the person may be required, including to take in or let out an item that does not fit precisely. Do ensure that if the person is taking in an item that there will be room for correction – an item that is too tight with no leeway will be unwearable.

In addition, aside from a handful of international schools, uniforms are still required for students and often parents will need to find the fabric and engage someone to produce them.

Drivers

Driving in Ghana is not for the faint of heart, requiring confidence and know-how. In addition, traffic in Greater Accra and Kumasi can be time-consuming, making appointments and errands significant time commitments. For these reasons and more, driving is a profession in itself.

There is a spectrum of drivers: first is the professional driver with a corporate vehicle. These are regularly engaged for offices, embassies and schools as well. These drivers are engaged by the organization, sometimes pool-managed[92] and are expected to keep the vehicles in

---

[91] Shopping for textiles at a Ghanaian market is a memorable experience for foreigners. Going with a tailor/seamstress can also ensure that you receive a fair market price and to check for quality – there is a brisk local trade in low-quality knock-off fabrics.

[92] Drivers managed in a pool are an example of an area where hidden office politics and hierarchies can surface. Who gets to drive whom and where? What about

tip-top shape, both in maintenance and regular cleaning. Next is the personal driver who is hired to drive the expat's vehicle. The same rules apply, although the employer has more direct say in matters and may need to keep a closer eye on maintenance and fuel levels. Finally, there are drivers with their own vehicles, in most cases taxis, hired ad-hoc, day-long or on a regular basis (e.g. travel to work, sending kids to school). Trusted drivers can even function as couriers and can run errands on their down-time.

Ghanaian taxis are the subject of an entire chapter, if not a book. Guide books will provide an overview of dropping and shared taxis. The bottom line is to know where you are going, how much it will cost to get there (haggling will be required) and to feel safe. Taxis are maintained in all sorts of ways, from pristine chariots to barely-roadworthy death traps. Some cars are their driver's pride and joy, while others simply exist to get people places as cheaply and profitably as possible. Taxis are also a source of crime. If travelling or sending a friend off at night, take note of the make, model and plate of the vehicle (and do so conspicuously) and text it to a third party. Ask the driver to take a particular route for your own peace of mind. In general, drivers may know the fastest/most efficient way, so if you are not sure, ask politely if they are taking an alternate route and don't question their intelligence (e.g. "Is this another route?" rather than, "Are you sure this is the way?").

The ideal driver should be a competent navigator, courteous and concerned for the safety and well-being of their passengers, especially if they are carrying groceries or small children. Their car should be well-maintained and clean. If you get a good taxi driver and car, ask for their number, either for your next trip or to recommend to friends and colleagues.

---

overtime opportunities and obtaining per diems?

Working with Ghanaians

Informal networks are also useful for people seeking drivers. Colleagues may have recommendations. On the formal side, hotels and offices may have recommended drivers, while the ride-sharing service Uber is available in Accra and Kumasi.

Drivers are overwhelmingly male, but more women are getting behind the wheel and crossing entrenched gender norms. Public transit company Metro Mass is increasingly hiring and training female drivers for their city buses as are other firms and organizations. There are also independent female taxi drivers. There is also an advantage for these drivers: Foreigners and female passengers in particular may feel safer and more at ease with a woman at the wheel.

Whomever the driver and whatever the purpose, the person should know how to operate and maintain the vehicle, know how to get you to your destination (including bypassing congestion and common bottlenecks) and do it safely.

Security Guards

An unfortunate reality of modern Ghana (particularly Accra) is that security guards are required to protect people and property at offices, shopping centres and compounds. Crime in Ghana is an issue and the police are not equipped to provide a rapid response. Thus, private security is a necessity for expats and a booming business. Guards provide 24/7 security and the first line of defence against criminal activity. That said, in Ghana, guards are typically uniformed men armed with only a flashlight, walkie-talkie and baton[93].

---

[93] Those coming from developed countries will find the presence of guards intrusive and excessive, while those coming from more insecure places may wonder if men without firearms or dogs can provide adequate security during a critical incident. As of the time of writing, Accra has not been subject to a large-scale terrorist attack nor are firearms widely available to criminals, so the security posture of guards are

Guards do not only deter would-be criminals at post and on patrol, but they can also coordinate the arrival of visitors and labourers, registering them and coordinating parking (essential in space-starved Accra). They also patrol the perimeter and look for security gaps, particularly during power outages. This all depends on the layout of the area, so ensure that your security detail is tailored to your needs. Your office will most likely engage a private security firm to contract and manage guards, so get to know their manager and have a frank discussion on your needs and ensure that they know your expectations. Female guards can be requested, particularly when visitors require searches, although they are typically only hired for daytime shifts. Ineffective guards can be reassigned elsewhere or fired for serious infractions.

Being a security guard requires little education and is not a particularly desirable profession. The combination of modest wages (as much as an entry-level police officer), long hours (12 hour shifts, six days per week) and sedentary nature of guarding (particularly at night) seem to encourage seeking of distractions, like side-jobs or napping, which is a serious issue when it comes to intruders[94]. Some security firms are experimenting with guards who have a five-day working week and a competitive salary, combined with a zero-tolerance policy. This sets a more rigorous work schedule, but also a more reasonable compensation package. Another recent phenomenon is hiring female guards, particularly for day shift work.

Informally, residential guards seem to do all sorts of general outdoor tasks: washing cars, providing simple yard maintenance and

---

relatively relaxed. The police and armed forces are well-armed and though not always quick to react, they are the ultimate guarantors of security.

[94] In one memorable example, intruders found a gap in a compound's security fence one night. The guard, who was a particularly heavy sleeper, was quietly relieved him of his cellphone, radio and locked in his hut until morning. It was only the security grills that prevented the houses from being entered. The guard was immediately relieved of duty, with cause.

whatever else may be asked (even urban farming, like growing and harvesting bananas on the compound!). Guards often do this to supplement their meager wages and to keep themselves occupied. However, expats should be very careful in engaging guards for household tasks, as it could keep them away from their post and could compromise their own security – or at least get them in trouble when their manager passes by for inspection. Any work should be done outside of shift hours.

As with domestic employees, it is best to keep a cordial, pleasant and arms-length relationship with residential guards. Their purpose is to provide security and to ensure that only desirable visitors enter (and should keep a log of them). They should have all equipment provided by the company, but ensure that they have access to clean water and a washroom. As the work is dull, providing a kettle, sugar and tea or instant coffee will earn you respect and keep your guards well-caffeinated. A small Christmas gift of provisions or occasional chop is always appreciated. Demands for extra work and loans are possible, so be prepared. If a guard solicits work unwantedly, sleeps on the job, is away from the post or makes the resident uncomfortable in any way, it is reasonable to ask for a new guard. Inversely, if moving, one can ask for a guard to be retained at the new site or for colleagues in need.

Movers

Those relocating to Ghana with a shipment will encounter a local moving company. These companies have extensive experience in packing and shipping. Teams are led by an experienced foreman supported by several day labourers, who may not be formal employees. Working with movers can be a multi-day process. The key is to communicate clearly any special needs for your items in packing or unpacking, like fragile items or items that need to be grouped together or specially marked. Sea shipment containers can experience condensation (known as *container rain* and *cargo sweat*), so insist on desiccant bags to absorb moisture and prevent water damage and mold. Sea containers should be sealed or unsealed in the presence of the customer for security and insurance purposes. To foster a respectful and diligent crew, providing cold water and chop is a good practice.

###

Acknowledgements and Resources

This started as a joke about a guide "that should be issued with the visa" and grew into a five-year side project spanning three continents. Thanks to my wife Maleaha for supporting and keeping me committed to this throughout. Thanks to my daughter Lena for her patience during the process and for her excitement in having an author and "explorer" for a father.

Thanks to my production consultant Dave Proctor for his high-level vision and editorial direction.

Thanks to Phil Baddoo, Esenam Nyador, Ron Quist, Dr. Joeva Rock, Darren Schemmer and Geoff Krauter for critical review of drafts and encouragement.

Thanks to author Glenn Brigaldino for sharing his e-publishing wisdom.

Thanks to Ngminvielu Kuuire for her fantastic cover design. https://ngminvielukuuire.wordpress.com/

Special thanks to the late Akua Akyaa Nkrumah for her inspiration and for showing how to effectively collaborate across cultures.

This project was inspired by the challenges of many obrunis and the frustrations of many Ghanaians who deal with them. Thanks to the many Ghanaian and non-Ghanaian respondents who took the time to provide insight and wisdom on how to better understand Ghanaian culture and to bridge intercultural gaps. Your interviews and correspondence have been essential to this project. If you see yourself in any part of this book, medase pa, thank you and merci.

Gye Nyame!

Essential reading

Briggs, Philip. Ghana: the Bradt Travel Guide. Eighth edition. The Globe Pequot Press Inc, 2019.

Prosper, Ivy. Your Essential Guide on Moving to Ghana. Second Edition. Independent. Accra. 2019.

Utley, Ian. Ghana – Culture Smart!: The Essential Guide to Customs & Culture. Second Edition. Kuperard, London. 2016.

North American Women's Association. No Worries! The Indispensable Guide to Ghana & Accra. Fifth Edition. 2013. Available online: http://noworriesghana.com

Works cited and general resources on Ghana

Damoah, Nana Awere. I Speak of Ghana. multiPIXEL Limited. Accra. 2013.

Sumprim, Alba Kunadu. The Imported Ghanaian. Mavrik. 2016.

Kuada, John and Yao Chachah. Ghana: Understanding the People and Their Culture. Woeli, 1999

Alexander, Max. Bright Lights, No City. First Edition. Hyperion, New York. 2012.

Konadu, Kwasi and Campbell, Clifford C (editors). The Ghana Reader: History, Culture, Politics. Duke University Press. 2016.

Kponor, Michael. Ghana's Best Guide to Pidgin English. Global Mamas, Accra. 2012.

Wanlov the Kubolor. The Corruption-Dumsor Mixtape. 2016. https://soundcloud.com/wanlov/sets/coraption-mixtape

Accra [dot] ALT. http://accradotaltradio.com

Other useful resources

Richmond, Yale and Gestrin, Phyllis. Into Africa: a Guide to Sub-Saharan Culture and Diversity. Second Edition. Intercultural Press. Boston. 2009.

Centre for Intercultural Learning, Canadian Foreign Service Institute. https://www.international.gc.ca/cil-cai/index.aspx?lang=eng

Vulpe, Thomas, Kealey, Daniel, Protheroe, David and Macdonald, Doug. A Profile of the Interculturally Effective Person. Centre for Intercultural Learning, Canadian Foreign Service Institute. Second Edition, 2001. Available online: https://www.international.gc.ca/cil-cai/publications.aspx?lang=eng

Janssen, Linda A. The Emotionally Resilient Expat. Summertime Publishing, 2013.

Covey, Steven. The Seven Habits of Highly Effective People. FranklinCovey, New York. 2013.

Robin, Vicki and Dominguez, Joe. Your Money or Your Life. Penguin, 2008.

Stone, Douglas, Patton, Bruce and Heen, Sheila. Difficult Conversations: How to Discuss What Matters Most. Penguin, 2010.

Hill, Declan. The Fix: Soccer and Organized Crime. McClelland and Stewart, Toronto. 2008.

Urech, Elzabeth. Speaking Globally. Kogan Page Ltd, London. 1997.

De Vries, Mary A. Internationally Yours: Writing and Communicating Successfully in Today's Global Marketplace. Houghton Mifflin Company, Boston. 1994.

About the Author

Michael Creighton is a Canadian who has spent several years living in Ghana as a university student and diplomat, including trips throughout via trotro, taxi, intercity bus and the occasional ferry, where he observed and engaged with countless Ghanaians from cocoa farmers to government ministers. He currently resides in Jerusalem with his family.

E-mail him at workingwithghanaians@gmail.com

Follow him on Twitter @misterobruni

www.ingramcontent.com/pod-product-compliance
Lightning Source LLC
Chambersburg PA
CBHW050001230526
45465CB00003BB/1207